QUILTING WITH STRIPS AND STRINGS

*With Complete Instructions
for Making 46 Patchwork Quilts*

Helen Whitson Rose

Dover Publications, Inc., New York

*Dedicated to
my sister Frances,
who gave help and encouragement
in all my quilting projects*

Edited by Linda Macho
Artwork by Janette Aiello
Book Design by Paula Goldstein

Published in Canada by General Publishing Company, Ltd., 30 Lesmill Road, Don Mills, Toronto, Ontario.
Published in the United Kingdom by Constable and Company, Ltd.

Quilting with Strips and Strings: With Complete Instructions for Making 46 Patchwork Quilts is a new work, first published by Dover Publications, Inc., in 1983.

Manufactured in the United States of America
Dover Publications, Inc., 180 Varick Street, New York, N.Y. 10014

Library of Congress Cataloging in Publication Data

Rose, Helen Whitson, 1917–
    Quilting with strips and strings.

    (Dover needlework series)
    1. Quilting.   I. Title.   II. Series.
TT835.R67   1983   746.46'041   82-4581
ISBN 0-486-24357-5   AACR2

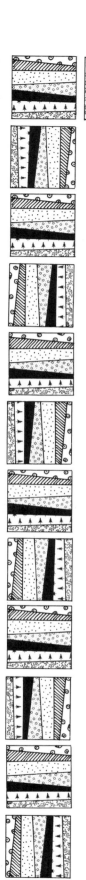

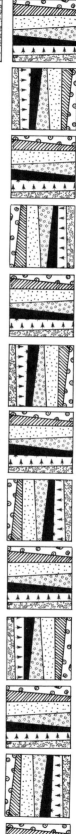

Introduction

Admirers of beautiful quilts have been heard to remark, "I'd like to be able to make a quilt someday, but I just don't have the patience to cut and sew all those little pieces together." Quilting with strips and strings is a perfect solution for those people with "no patience" and for those who wish to add a new dimension to their quilting skills. This book contains many intricate-looking designs which have been simplified so that beautiful results can be achieved with a minimal amount of work and time.

Now you may ask, "What is the difference between a strip and a string?" I have never read a better definition than that given by Bonnie Leman in the March 1982 issue of *Quilter's Newsletter Magazine,* and she has graciously agreed to allow me to include it in this introduction.

> The term "string" originally referred to the long, narrow strips of fabric left over from cutting a garment, strips that would ordinarily be too narrow to be of any useful purpose. Frugal quiltmakers have long made quilts from these strings, usually sewing them onto a paper or muslin base so they could be joined into a quilt top. In most string quilts no effort was made to trim the strings symmetrically, since they were already so narrow. Instead they often joined in a random, crazy-quilt effect. In the '20s and '30s several quilt designs evolved from the random string quilt, among them *String Star* and *Spider Web*. For these designs the strings were sewn onto a base (paper or cloth) which had been pre-cut into a specific shape. The finished string shapes were then joined to create pieced blocks or units of the quilt top.

> "Strip" piecing is like string piecing in that it utilizes strips of fabric which are sewn together. However, unlike string piecing, the width and color of the strips are planned. Strip piecing is more versatile than string piecing. New "yardage" can be made from strips from which template shapes can be cut, the yardage can be cut apart and rearranged, the strips may be sewn on a foundation pre-cut to shape, or any combination thereof.

Construction on the sewing machine is highly recommended; however, handwork can and should be used if that is your preference. There are several ways to quilt with strips and strings; I have covered three major techniques in this book: making string material (pages 6–9), assembling strings the old-fashioned way on a fabric or paper base (pages 9—10) and assembling strings on a lining and batting so you are quilting and sewing at the same time (pages 10–12—"Quilt-As-You-Go"). Each method is described in detail with clear diagrams—it is up to you to select the method you wish to use when making your strip and string projects. The rest of the book is filled with designs; most are very easy, some are a challenge, but all will show you the versatility and fun of quilting with strips and strings.

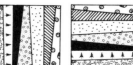

EQUIPMENT

It is wise to assemble all the necessary equipment *before* beginning a project; this will not only save time, but will also ensure greater accuracy in your work (you won't be tempted to "short cut" a step just because you don't have the right piece of equipment at hand). Keep your supplies organized and in one place; this will enable you to pick up your work whenever you have a spare moment. A medium-size basket or box would be suitable for storage of most equipment; templates should be stored in labelled envelopes. Following is a list of the equipment needed for string quilting.

Pencils

Use sharp, soft-lead pencils for ruling lines on fabric and for tracing around templates; *never* use ink when marking fabrics! If you are using dark fabrics or fabrics with a busy print, use tailor's chalk or light-colored marking pencils.

Shears

Sharp dressmaker's shears are needed for cutting several layers of fabric at one time. You will also need scissors for cutting paper; using your best shears to cut paper templates will dull them in a hurry. Small embroidery scissors are excellent for cutting away excess threads.

Pins

Pins should be rust-proof and perfectly straight. Pins with plastic heads are easy to work with and are less likely to be accidentally left in the fabric.

Measuring Devices

A wooden yardstick and a 12"–15" ruler are necessary for string quilting; both should be in good condition and free from nicks. A tape measure will also be necessary, particularly for making string material.

Iron

Ironing is necessary for professional results and is an essential part of almost every step of the piecing process. It is best to use an iron with a steam setting; if this is not possible, pressing with a damp cloth will suffice.

Needles

Needles will be necessary for any hand sewing or appliqué work; use "Sharps," which are medium-length sewing needles. Use quilting needles called "Betweens" in sizes 7–9 for any hand quilting that may need to be done.

Sewing Machine

Although string quilting can be done by hand, it is recommended that a sewing machine be used; this will save a great deal of time and will result in an item that can stand up to much wear. The sewing machine needs no special attachments, but it should be able to stitch forward and in reverse; a basting stitch would be an asset. A presser foot with a ¼" strip of metal on each side of the needle slot is ideal for gauging seams in strip piecing as well as patchwork; a ¼" seam allowance is standard for all patterns. If such a presser foot cannot be obtained, place a piece of tape on the machine plate ¼" away from the needle as a guide for sewing ¼" seams.

Template Supplies

When working a design that requires a shaped piece, a template must be made. You will need tracing paper, a pencil, scissors, glue and medium-weight cardboard. Trace the pattern from the book, marking both the stitching and cutting lines along with the pattern name, template number (where applicable) and grainline. Cut out the tracing paper pattern, then glue that thin pattern onto medium-weight cardboard. Cut out the cardboard pattern. If desired, strengthen the edges of the pattern by coating with several layers of clear nail polish. **Hint:** To prevent slippage when cutting out fabric pieces, glue the template to sandpaper so the rough side will be placed on the fabric when marking or cutting.

Thimble

The thimble is an excellent aid for hand sewing and will save wear and tear on your finger. The fit should be snug and the thimble long enough to come to the first joint of the middle finger. If you find it uncomfortable to use a thimble, a piece of adhesive tape on the tip of your middle finger will protect it.

Thread

Use a color-fast thread in a matching or neutral color. Any high-quality mercerized cotton or polyester thread will be suitable. Cotton thread may shrink when washed and cause unwanted puckers in the fabric. It is advisable to use a cotton-covered polyester thread if the quilt is going to be laundered frequently; this thread will also prevent static build-up in the needle of the sewing machine.

Batting

When the quilt is ready to be assembled or when using the quilt-as-you-go method (see pages 10–12), batting is used between the top and the lining to give warmth and loft to the finished quilt. Batting can be cotton or polyester. I recommend using polyester batting because it is machine-washable, will dry quickly without lumping, and is available in large, pre-cut seamless sheets.

Decide if your project needs a puffy or a flat look, and choose your batting loft accordingly: the felted-type batting (⅛"-thick) is suitable for garments, craft projects and quilt-as-you-go projects; the glazed, loftier batting is ideal for hand quilting and quilt-as-you-go projects; substantial batting (½"-thick or more) is excellent for hand-tied quilts, and gives quite a puffy effect. Batting is readily available in fabric shops, department, hobby and craft stores or through mail order from quilt supply companies.

SELECTING AND PREPARING FABRICS

Ideally, you should have many scraps and remnants of fabric from other quilting and sewing projects that can be used for string quilting. When going through your "rag bag," look for fabrics that have good, firm body but are not too heavy. 100% cotton fabrics such as calico, percale, broadcloth, muslin and gingham work best, although a small percentage of polyester in cotton fabric will increase the washability of the finished quilt.

After you have sorted your scraps and selected the pieces you wish to use, divide the fabrics into color families, and then divide the families into solids and prints. You are now in a position to decide upon the overall color scheme of the quilt, and can make a judgment about the fabrics you will need to buy. Do you have a preponderance of solid color fabrics? Then it would be wise to buy an array of prints in matching colors for a pleasing balance. Do you notice a large number of dull prints? Then you may wish to purchase some bright solids to add snap to your quilt. You may decide to make a multicolor quilt with a random color scheme in the same manner as the crazy quilts of the Victorian era. This is fine, but some of the designs in this book require pieces of a certain color or in a special arrangement for the final effect; for these designs, you may have to buy new fabrics.

Figuring Yardage

Yardage has not been given for most of the patterns in this book because of the nature of string quilting—meaning that you are expected to use scraps and remnants. However, you will probably need to figure yardage for some of the major pieces for which templates are given, and for sashing (if desired) and lining (which is required). Yardage can be quickly and easily calculated following the directions below and the section called "Quick Cuts from Strips" on page 6.

(1) Following *Figures 3–9* on pages 6–7 for template placement, count the number of pieces that can be placed on one quarter yard of fabric (18 pieces fit in the example used below).

(2) Multiply the number of pieces by four to get the number of pieces that can be cut from one yard of fabric (18 × 4 = 72 pieces).

(3) Count the number of pieces required for the size quilt you are going to make, for example:

$$
\begin{array}{r}
48 \\
\times\ 4 \\
\hline
192
\end{array}
$$

48   blocks in quilt
× 4   pieces required for each block
192   total number of pieces needed for quilt

(4) Divide the number of pieces cut from one yard of fabric (72) into the total number of pieces needed for the entire quilt (192) for the total yardage for one pattern piece, for example:

$$
\begin{array}{r}
2 \text{ yds.} \\
72\overline{)192} \\
144 \\
\hline
48
\end{array}
$$

48 pieces which need to be cut from the next yard

In this case it would be wise to buy three yards of fabric to allow for the remaining 48 pieces and for straightening grain and cutting strips and strings to make up other pieces in the quilt.

Follow this method to estimate yardage for any other large pieces in the quilt. Sometimes yardage for other pieces can be judged from your first calculation, to save time, however, always purchase more fabric than you think you'll need because dye lots can vary and additional fabric may not be available when you need it. Keep in mind that a quilt top requires from five to ten yards of fabric, depending upon the size of the quilt and the number of seams and pieces. Additional fabric may be needed for sashing between the blocks, for a border and for the lining. Check the width of the fabric you have chosen and make your yardage estimates as described above.

Final Preparations

After your fabric selection has been made and you have bought all the new material you'll need, pre-wash everything in hot water. This will shrink the fabric and remove any sizing that may be present. Also, red and dark blue fabrics tend to bleed if the original dyeing was done carelessly; pre-washing will reduce the possibility of a disaster after the quilt top has been completed. **Note:** Be sure to separate the darks from the lights when pre-washing! Place small scraps or strips in a mesh bag to prevent tangling in washing.

Air- or machine-dry the fabric, then carefully press all the pieces before you begin to work. When pressing, check the grain line carefully. Lengthwise threads should be parallel to the selvage and crosswise threads should be exactly perpendicular to the selvage to ensure that the pieces will be correctly cut. If the fabric seems off-grain, pull it to straighten. It helps if two people work on this (although you can do it by yourself); have each person hold a corner of the fabric. Stretch the fabric along the true bias in the direction opposite the off-grain edge by pulling the fabric from opposite corners. Pull several times until the crosswise threads are at right angles to the lengthwise threads, then press.

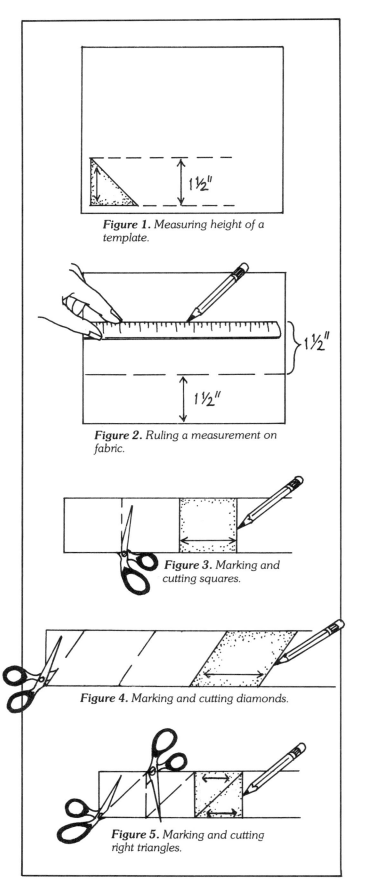

Figure 1. *Measuring height of a template.*

Figure 2. *Ruling a measurement on fabric.*

Figure 3. *Marking and cutting squares.*

Figure 4. *Marking and cutting diamonds.*

Figure 5. *Marking and cutting right triangles.*

QUICK CUTS FROM STRIPS

Here are some ways to hasten the job of cutting a large number of like fabric pieces for a quilt top. These methods will also save fabric and will enable you to easily figure the required yardage (see ''Figuring Yardage'' on page 5).

(1) Make a template of the pattern piece from cardboard, sandpaper or thin plastic (see page 4—Template Supplies); be sure a ¼″ seam allowance has been added on all sides. Mark the pattern piece number and the grainline on the template.

(2) Prepare the fabric following directions on page 5. Place the fabric on a large table or flat surface, making sure the grain is straight and the fabric lies smoothly in place.

(3) Position the template correctly on the fabric (following the grainline), then measure the height of the template on the fabric *(Figure 1)*. Remove the template and rule this measurement across the fabric with a yardstick and pencil *(Figure 2)*.

(4) Cut out strips of fabric along the ruled lines, then stack three or four strips together, edges matching, and pin carefully.

(5) Position the appropriate template on the stack of strips as shown in *Figures 3–9* and draw cutting lines with a ruler where two pieces touch. Using very sharp fabric shears, cut pieces apart on ruled lines, making only one cut to separate two pieces.

(6) Stack like pieces together and sew through the stack with a long thread knotted at one end. Wrap the free end of the thread in a figure-eight around a pin in the top layers of the stack for easy removal of the pieces when needed.

For clarity, the examples in *Figures 3–9* illustrate the cutting of patchwork pieces from unpieced fabrics. However, the same techniques apply to cutting patchwork pieces from string material as well (see ''Making String Material'' below). It is important that the string material be carefully pressed before cutting so there are no puckers. When cutting patchwork pieces from string material *(Figure 10),* cut only one layer at a time; this will ensure accuracy.

MAKING STRING MATERIAL

String material is a fabric composed of long strips of material that have been pieced and sewn together. By making string material, normally unusable or waste pieces of fabric can be combined to create a usable piece of fabric which can then be cut into different shapes. The fabric strips composing string material do not have to be a uniform width. In fact, using strips of different widths will add interest and excitement to the finished piece of string material. Color will also play a tremendous role in the ultimate appearance of the string material. Reflect

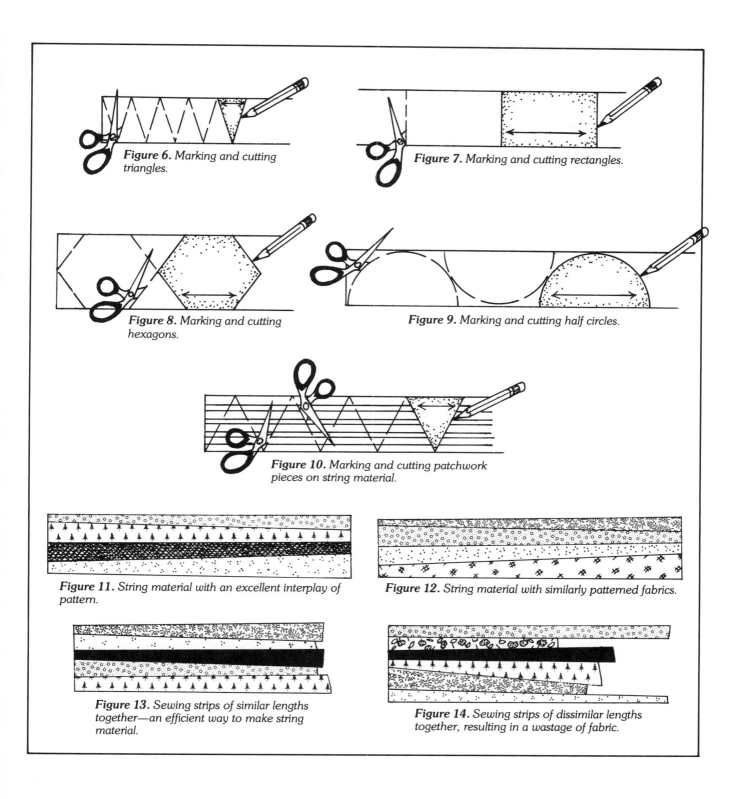

Figure 6. *Marking and cutting triangles.*

Figure 7. *Marking and cutting rectangles.*

Figure 8. *Marking and cutting hexagons.*

Figure 9. *Marking and cutting half circles.*

Figure 10. *Marking and cutting patchwork pieces on string material.*

Figure 11. *String material with an excellent interplay of pattern.*

Figure 12. *String material with similarly patterned fabrics.*

Figure 13. *Sewing strips of similar lengths together—an efficient way to make string material.*

Figure 14. *Sewing strips of dissimilar lengths together, resulting in a wastage of fabric.*

carefully on the placement of adjacent fabrics and colors as you sew the strips together. For example, you can use light next to dark, dull next to bright and print next to solid. As you can see in *Figure 11,* fabrics with different patterns will complement each other more than fabrics with the same kind of overall pattern *(Figure 12).*

The width of a piece of string material is dictated by the length of the fabric strips used to construct it. To be efficient, gather together your long strips of fabric, then divide the strips into groups of similar length. Sew these groups together to eliminate waste in the finished width; see *Figures 13* and *14.* You will end up with several different widths of string material, all of which will be totally usable.

After you have decided upon a color/print scheme and after you have divided your strips into groups by length, construct your string material as follows: With right sides of the strips facing one another, sew the pieces together making 12 stitches-per-inch on your sewing machine (if sewing by hand, make very tiny stitches). Different effects can be achieved by rotating the fabric strips slightly as you join them. For normal sewing, you are usually instructed to "sew pieces together with raw edges even making ¼" seams." This does not necessarily apply to string material, although you can sew your strips together in this way if you want an even, structured look; in several cases, a structured look is required for a specific type of patchwork design such as *London Stairs* on page 15 or *Rail Fence* on page 18. However, to add some energy and interest to string material that does not have to be structured, you may want to adjust your strips so the raw edges are *not* even before sewing them together *(Figure 15)*. If this is done carefully, you will end up with a fabric that looks more intriguing than a structured piece of fabric; see *Figure 16*.

Sew strips of similar-length fabric together until you have reached the desired size of string material; keep in mind that the size of the material will increase considerably after pressing. Next, press the string material using steam if possible. Press all seam allowances *to one side,* preferably toward the darker fabric. Pressing the seam allowances to one side strengthens the seam (be sure that you do not crease or pleat the seam when pressing to one side). Also press on the right side to remove any pleats or tucks.

String material can be used in many ways. You can use it as a background fabric for a simple appliqué design *(Figure 17)*. Conversely, use the string material to cut out an appliqué, then sew it to a solid background fabric *(Figure 18)*. You can cut the string material into blocks, then sew the blocks together to create a design *(Figure 19)*; Chapter 1 deals with this type of usage. Blocks of

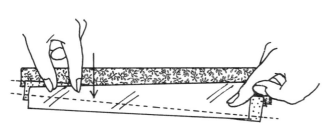

Figure 15. Rotating strips slightly before sewing.

Structured string material.

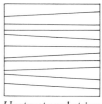

Unstructured string material.

Figure 16.

Figure 17. Using string material as a background for appliqué.

Figure 18. Using string material to make an appliqué.

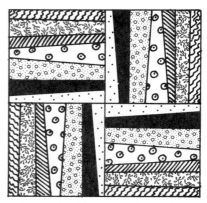

Figure 19. Creating a design from blocks of string material.

string material can be alternated with solid blocks of fabric to create a totally different type of design (Figure 20). An attractive edging can also be made from string material. First construct a wide piece of the string material, then mark the desired width of the edging plus ½" for seam allowances on the material using a ruler and pencil. Cut out the strips along the marked lines (Figure 21); strips can be joined to make any length of edging that is required. A string edging can add a distinctive finishing touch to a simple quilt or pillow (Figure 22); it can also be used on collars, cuffs, yokes and hems to enhance a garment. Patchwork pieces of all shapes and sizes can be cut from string material; see "Quick Cuts from Strings" on pages 6–7, Figures 3–10.

ASSEMBLING STRINGS ON A BASE

Quilters may make and use string material as described on pages 6–8 and find that they would prefer to work with a fabric that has a firmer body and less "give"; if this is the case, strips can be assembled on a fabric or paper base. For complicated designs where patchwork pieces must match perfectly, strings should be assembled on a base that has been cut from a template. When using the quilt-as-you-go method (see pages 10–12) the blocks are assembled on batting and a fabric base. A fabric or paper base is also required when making any of the designs in the *Log Cabin* family; this is discussed in detail in Chapter 2. The following directions explain the basic techniques for sewing strips to a base.

For a fabric base, use lightweight material that is compatible in fiber content with the strips you will be applying to it; this will eliminate any problems with shrinkage when the finished item is washed. If using a paper base, use plain brown paper or newspaper that is at least six weeks old (to prevent the newsprint from smearing onto the fabric). The size and shape of the base will depend upon what you are making. If making string material, the base should be as wide as the longest strip of fabric. For patchwork pieces that are to be covered with strings, the base must include a ¼" seam allowance all around.

The illustrations that follow feature a triangle base, but the technique is the same for all base shapes. Directions for sewing *Log Cabin* designs to a base are given in Chapter 2 on pages 32–33, and will not be covered here.

Cut out the base to the desired size using a template (or measuring carefully with a pencil and ruler); if applicable, mark the sewing line ¼" away from the edge of the fabric on the *wrong side*. Place the base on a flat surface, *right side up,* then place the first strip, right side up, on the base so the edges extend slightly beyond the base on each side (Figure 23); trim away the excess fabric (if necessary) as shown. Place a second strip over the first with right sides facing and pin in place along one edge; trim if necessary. Sew both strips to the base along

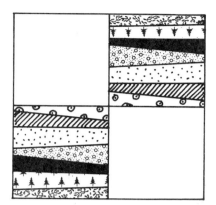

Figure 20. Alternating blocks of solid and string material.

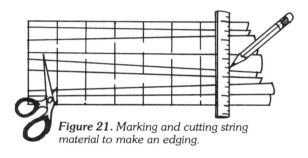

Figure 21. Marking and cutting string material to make an edging.

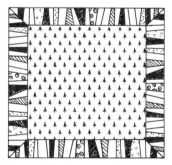

Figure 22. A string edging can enhance a quilt or pillow.

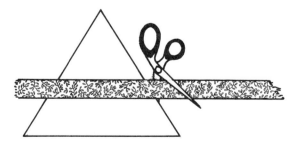

Figure 23. Place the first strip, right side up, on the base, trimming away excess fabric if necessary.

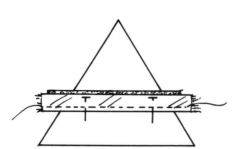

Figure 24. Pin the second strip over the first, right sides facing, and sew in place.

Figure 25. Press the second strip open.

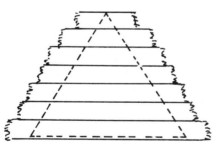

Figure 26. Add strips to each side of the first strip until the entire base is covered.

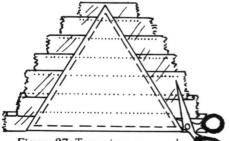

Figure 27. Turn piece over and cut away excess fabric even with edge of patchwork piece.

pinned edge *(Figure 24)* making sure that all pieces remain flat and smooth as they feed through the presser foot of the sewing machine. Remove pins, then press the second strip to the right side *(Figure 25)*. Continue adding strips to each side of the first strip until the entire base is covered, pressing after the addition of each strip *(Figure 26)*. Turn piece to wrong side and trim away excess fabric even with the edge of the base *(Figure 27)*. The sewing lines will be visible on the wrong side. If using a paper base, pull fabric on the bias in the direction opposite the rows of stitching, then gently tear away the paper without distorting the sewn fabric. Press carefully on both sides.

QUILT-AS-YOU-GO

Quilt-as-you-go is a method for quilting individual blocks by hand or machine. If this method is done by hand, the quilt blocks can be carried around with you to be worked on during spare moments; also, the work can be held quite close to where you are quilting, enabling you to make small stitches. If done by machine, a quilt can be completed almost while it is being sewn because you are quilting and sewing at the same time; also, the work is not as bulky as when you are working with a complete quilt where an entire padded quilt top would have to pass under the head of the sewing machine.

This method does have some limitations. The actual quilting design must not come closer than ¼″ from the edge of the block because there must be sufficient free fabric to join the blocks at the edges. Joining the blocks is a tedious process which entails stitching the pieced blocks together, whip-stitching the batting together, then lapping and hand-sewing the lining in place. However, the saving of time in the actual quilting and the convenience of this method may more than make up for the time it will take to assemble the blocks.

Before quilting by this method, read the section called "Assembling Strings on a Base" on page 9; the actual sewing techniques are the same, although for the quilt-as-you-go method, the base fabric (and you must use fabric rather than paper) will be the lining, so select it with care. Also, because most batting today is polyester, which will melt under high heat, the pieces are *not ironed* after they have been stitched in place; rather, "finger press" the pieces by turning them back and running the tip of your index finger over the seam several times. Follow the directions below for this simple, modern method of quilting.

(1) Cut a lining (base) ¼″ larger all around than the size given for the finished block.

(2) Cut a layer of batting ¼″ smaller all around than the lining; pin the batting, centered, on the lining. Baste the batting to the lining diagonally from corner to corner or horizontally and vertically *(Figure 28);* basting lines will cross in exact center of lining and will serve as placement lines for patchwork pieces, if needed. Remove pins.

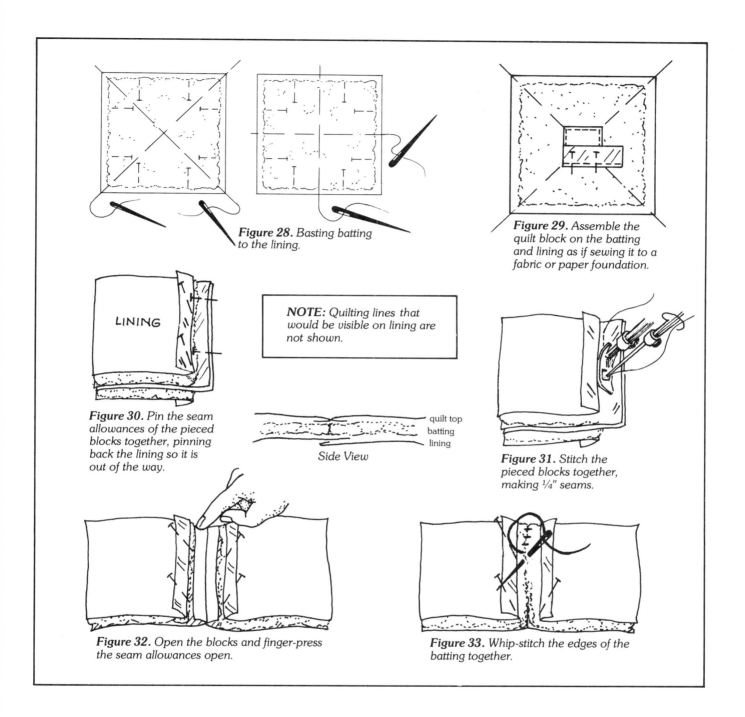

Figure 28. Basting batting to the lining.

Figure 29. Assemble the quilt block on the batting and lining as if sewing it to a fabric or paper foundation.

LINING

NOTE: Quilting lines that would be visible on lining are not shown.

Figure 30. Pin the seam allowances of the pieced blocks together, pinning back the lining so it is out of the way.

quilt top
batting
lining

Side View

Figure 31. Stitch the pieced blocks together, making ¼″ seams.

Figure 32. Open the blocks and finger-press the seam allowances open.

Figure 33. Whip-stitch the edges of the batting together.

(3) Following the individual directions for each patchwork design, assemble the quilt block on the batting and lining as if sewing the pieces to a plain fabric or paper foundation (Figure 29). When stitching outer pieces in place, end stitching ¼″ from end of strip or piece; for machine stitching, pull thread ends to the top side of the block and knot before clipping away excess.

(4) After the necessary number of blocks have been completed, arrange them all on a large flat surface to determine placement. When you are satisfied with the arrangement, the blocks can be sewn together.

(5) Pin the seam allowances of the pieced blocks together (top layer), holding or pinning back the lining fabric and batting to keep them out of the way (Figure 30). Stitch the pieced blocks together by hand or machine (machine stitching is illustrated) following Figure 31 and making ¼″ seams.

(6) Open the blocks and finger-press the seam allowances open (Figure 32).

(7) The batting from each block will meet exactly over the seam allowance; whip-stitch the edges together (Figure 33).

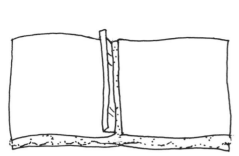

Figure 34. *Smooth one lining over the batting; fold raw edge of other lining ¼″ to wrong side.*

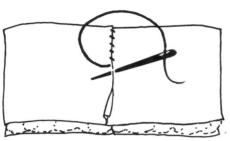

Figure 35. *Slip-stitch lining in place.*

(8) Remove the pins holding the lining in place; smooth one lining straight over the batting and finger-press the raw edge of the other lining ¼″ to the wrong side *(Figure 34).*

(9) Slip-stitch the folded edge of the lining in place, being careful not to catch the quilt top *(Figure 35).*

(10) After all the blocks have been joined in horizontal rows, follow the directions above to join the rows, being careful to match the seams on the quilt top when sewing the rows together. The outer edges of the quilt can be bound in any way you wish.

CREATING A QUILT WITH STRIP AND STRING DESIGNS

To determine the number of blocks needed to create any one quilt in this book, make a rough estimate of the size of the quilt you wish to construct; draw this measurement to scale on graph paper. Select the design you wish to make and find the block size given for that design; block sizes do not include seam allowances. Using that measurement, draw blocks to scale on your graph paper, fitting as many blocks as possible within the space you have drawn. Chances are that the blocks will not fit exactly, but you can always add borders or stripping, or simply make the quilt slightly smaller or larger than you had first estimated. Count the number of blocks in your diagram to determine how many you will need to make. Some string designs given in this book are constructed from strips rather than blocks; for those designs, the quilt can be made to your exact specifications providing that you carefully plan strip sizes and borders in advance. Read the individual directions carefully, then work out your measurements on graph paper before beginning.

Since complete instructions for quiltmaking are provided in most of the many wonderful quilting books on the market today, I have deliberately omitted covering that subject in depth in this book. Following is a list of books that I consider to be the best on this subject; all will contain excellent information on quiltmaking.

Selected Bibliography of Quilting Books

BONESTEEL, GEORGIA. *Lap Quilting With Georgia Bonesteel.* Oxmoor House, P.O. Box 463, Birmingham, AL 35201.

LEMAN, BONNIE, AND MARTIN, JUDY. *Log Cabin Quilts.* Moon Over the Mountain Publishing Company, 6700 West 4th Avenue, Denver, CO 80033.

LEONE, DIANA. *The Sampler Quilt.* Leone Publications, 2721 Lyle Court, Santa Clara, CA 95051.

PUCKETT, MARJORIE, AND GIBERSON, GAIL. *Primarily Patchwork.* Cabin Craft, Box 561, Redlands, CA 92373.

WEISS, RITA. *Easy-to-Make Patchwork Quilts.* Dover Publications, Inc., 180 Varick Street, New York, NY 10014.

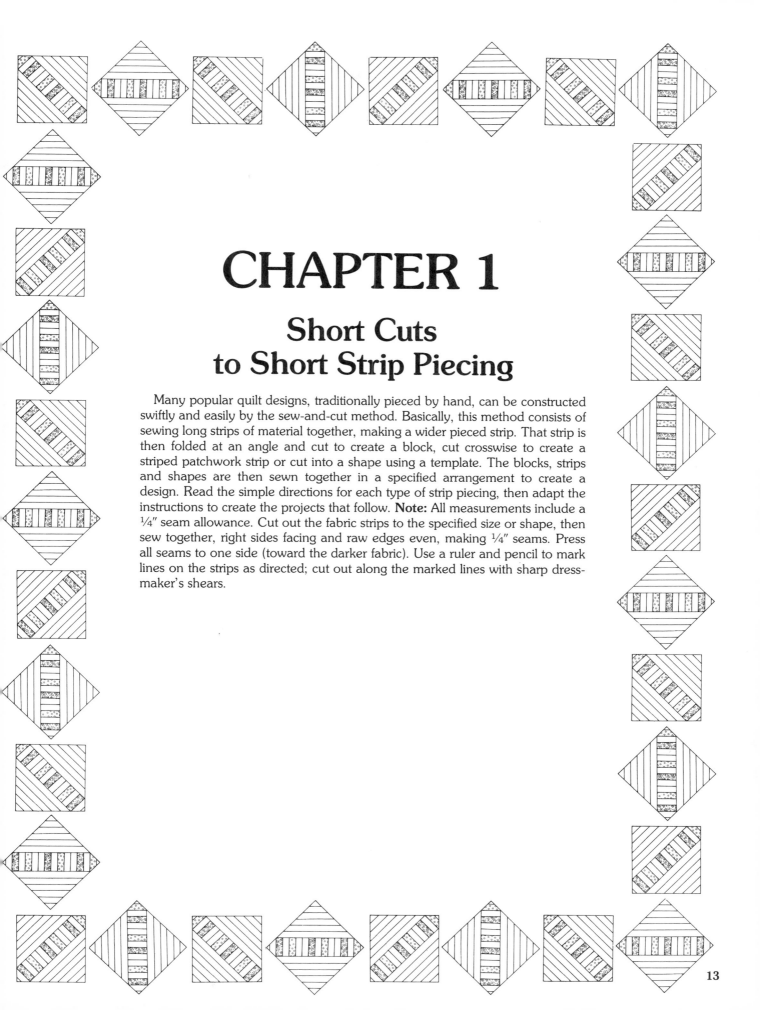

CHAPTER 1

Short Cuts
to Short Strip Piecing

Many popular quilt designs, traditionally pieced by hand, can be constructed swiftly and easily by the sew-and-cut method. Basically, this method consists of sewing long strips of material together, making a wider pieced strip. That strip is then folded at an angle and cut to create a block, cut crosswise to create a striped patchwork strip or cut into a shape using a template. The blocks, strips and shapes are then sewn together in a specified arrangement to create a design. Read the simple directions for each type of strip piecing, then adapt the instructions to create the projects that follow. **Note:** All measurements include a ¼″ seam allowance. Cut out the fabric strips to the specified size or shape, then sew together, right sides facing and raw edges even, making ¼″ seams. Press all seams to one side (toward the darker fabric). Use a ruler and pencil to mark lines on the strips as directed; cut out along the marked lines with sharp dress-maker's shears.

STRIP PIECING TO FORM BLOCKS

Following *Figure 36* for different fabric combinations, cut long strips to the specified width (an average width is 2½″) and sew together in groups of 2, 3, 4, 5 or 6 (groups of 3 are illustrated here; groups of six are illustrated on the front cover). Following *Figure 37,* "square off" the pieced strip by folding the fabric edge on the diagonal as shown. Mark the right edge of the diagonally folded fabric, then cut along the vertical line, forming a square block. Use this square as a pattern to cut the rest of the squares. Strips of any width and number can be sewn together and squared off by this method. Assemble the squares into a random design or into one of the traditional designs on the following pages.

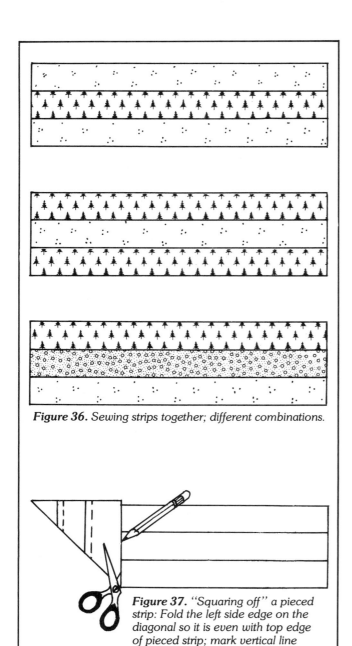

Figure 36. Sewing strips together; different combinations.

Figure 37. "Squaring off" a pieced strip: Fold the left side edge on the diagonal so it is even with top edge of pieced strip; mark vertical line along right edge, then cut out on marked line.

London Stairs

Block Size: 4″ square.

This easiest of patchwork patterns is made from two strips of fabric, one light and one dark, each 2½″ wide. Sew one light and one dark strip together, then square off and cut into blocks. Alternate the vertical and horizontal placement of the blocks to form a zigzag design as shown.

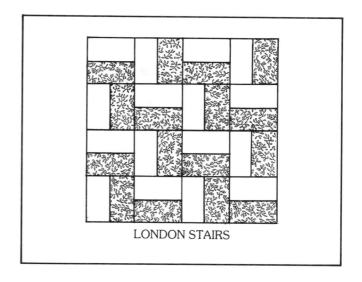

LONDON STAIRS

Basket Weave

Block Size: 6″ square.

Basket Weave is made from two contrasting fabrics that are cut into 2½″-wide strips and then sewn into groups of three. Group A should have a light fabric in the center, bordered on each side by a strip of dark fabric; group B should have a dark fabric in the center, bordered on each side by a strip of light fabric. Sew the three strips together forming equal amounts of group A and group B, then square off and cut into blocks. Following the illustration, arrange the blocks to form a basket weave design, alternating group A and group B as shown.

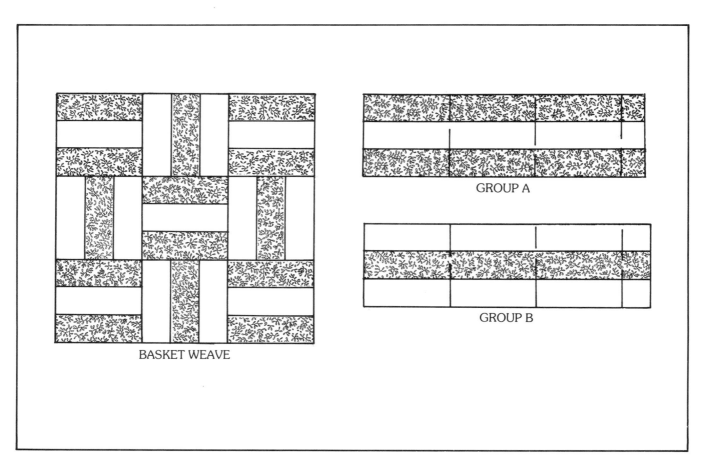

BASKET WEAVE

GROUP A

GROUP B

Roman Stripe

Block Size: 6″ square.

This design is also known as *Spirit of St. Louis* or *Interlocked Squares* and can be made from assorted fabrics cut in 2½″-wide strips; the design will have greater unity if the prints harmonize, or if all of the fabrics are in harmonizing colors. Sew three strips together in random color arrangements, then square off and cut into blocks. Alternate the vertical and horizontal placement of the blocks to form the design shown.

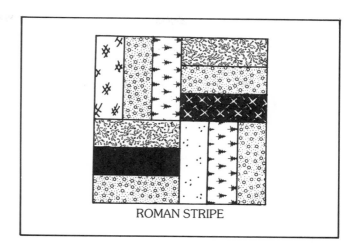

ROMAN STRIPE

Five Stripe

Block Size: 7½″ square.

This design is created by cutting three different prints and two different solids into 2″-wide strips. Sew the strips together, alternating solids and prints as shown in the *Five Stripe Diagram.* Cut into blocks; assemble the blocks following the photograph.

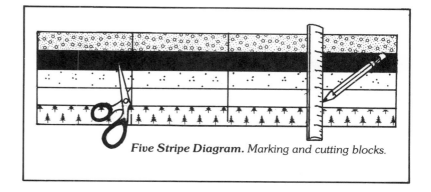

Five Stripe Diagram. Marking and cutting blocks.

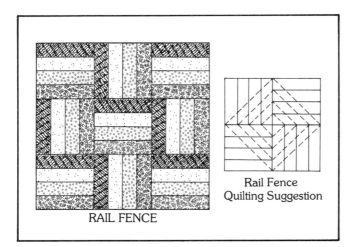

Rail Fence
Quilting Suggestion

RAIL FENCE

Rail Fence

Block Size: 11″ square.

Rail Fence can be achieved by sewing four strips together, each 3¼″ wide, using the same bold but coordinating fabric on the outside each time. Square off the pieced strip and cut into blocks. When assembling the blocks, alternate the vertical and horizontal placement, arranging the bold strip to form a *Rail Fence* zigzag design as shown. Follow the quilting suggestion for a lovely geometric effect.

STRIP PIECING TO FORM BRICKWORK DESIGNS

Sew wide strips of fabric together in alternating color and print combinations. Strips should measure from 3½″ to 7½″ wide; the width of the strips will dictate the width of each "brick." Press the seams to one side. Using a yardstick and pencil, rule across the pieced fabric the desired height of the bricks as shown in *Figure 38;* a good rule of thumb is that the height should be about half the width of the bricks. This height measurement should also include an extra ½″ for seam allowances. Cut along the ruled lines as shown. Following the sample designs, rearrange the strips in the desired pattern, then sew together, making ¼″ seams.

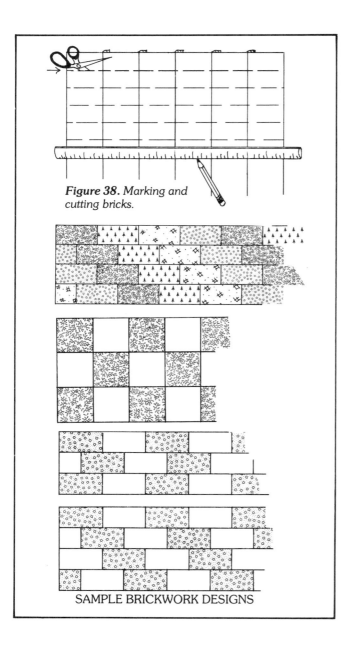

Figure 38. Marking and cutting bricks.

SAMPLE BRICKWORK DESIGNS

STRIP PIECING TO CREATE ROMAN STRIPE VARIATIONS

Roman Stripe is a simple design that can be made from scrap fabrics in several variations other than the traditional style discussed on page 17. The design can be made to any size, and the width and number of horizontal, vertical and diagonal strips can be adjusted to proportions suitable for a quilt or a pillow. Machine sewing is recommended for quick and easy completion.

Vertical Roman Stripe

Following the diagram, sew fabric strips of random width and color together for the vertical pieced sections (S), either by making string material (page 6) or by sewing the strips to a fabric or paper base (page 9). Trim the edges of the strips evenly making sections of equal width, then cut vertical stripping about 2½″ wide (V) and sew to each side of the pieced sections. Add a 2½″ border at the top and bottom (B) to complete the quilt or pillow top.

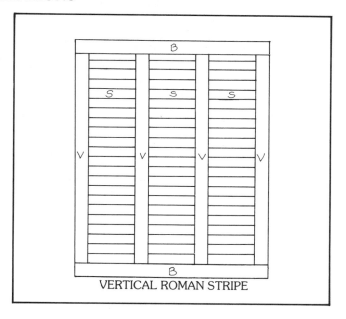
VERTICAL ROMAN STRIPE

Roman Stripes and Squares

This design is a variation of *Vertical Roman Stripe*. Make string material as shown in *Roman Diagram*, alternating narrow and wide strips as illustrated. Measure height of wide strips, add ½″ (for seam allowances) and rule that measurement on the string material. Cut out; wide strips will become squares when joined with vertical stripping. An attractive design will result if the vertical stripping is cut to the same width as the narrow strips comprising the string material.

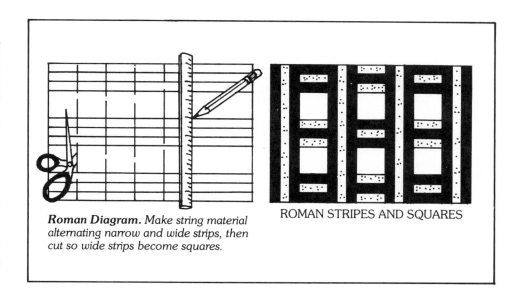

Roman Diagram. Make string material alternating narrow and wide strips, then cut so wide strips become squares.

ROMAN STRIPES AND SQUARES

Roman Square

Block Size: 16″ square.

All strips must be the same width when making a *Roman Square*. Cut six strips, each 2½″ × 12½″; sew together forming the center section. Cut two strips, each 2½″ × 12½″; sew to each side of pieced section as shown. Cut two strips, each 2½″ × 16½″; sew to top and bottom of block. There is a ¼″ seam allowance all around edge of block for sewing to other blocks or to a backing if making a pillow top.

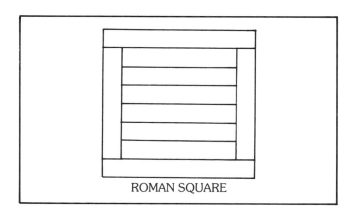
ROMAN SQUARE

Diagonal Roman Stripe

This design is achieved by sewing four blocks together, each block being a square cut on the diagonal from the *Vertical Roman Stripe* design. Follow the diagrams and directions below to create this striking design. **Hint:** These four squares would make a pretty center for a medallion quilt.

Decide upon the size square you wish to make; divide that square into four equal parts *(Diagonal Diagram 1)*. Make a cardboard template for that quarter measurement plus ½″ for seam allowances; measure the template diagonally *(Diagonal Diagram 2)*. Make two rows of *Vertical Roman Stripe* (see page 19) the height of the diagonal measurement; use two rows of stripping as shown in *Diagonal Diagram 3*. For length, multiply the diagonal measurement by four, i.e. 12″ × 4 = 48″ total length. Place the cardboard template on the pieced fabric as shown, carefully lining up the points of the square on the center seam; mark the outline with a pencil, then cut along the marked line, cutting four squares in total *(Diagonal Diagram 4)*. Sew the four squares together as shown in the illustration, making ¼″ seams and matching seams carefully.

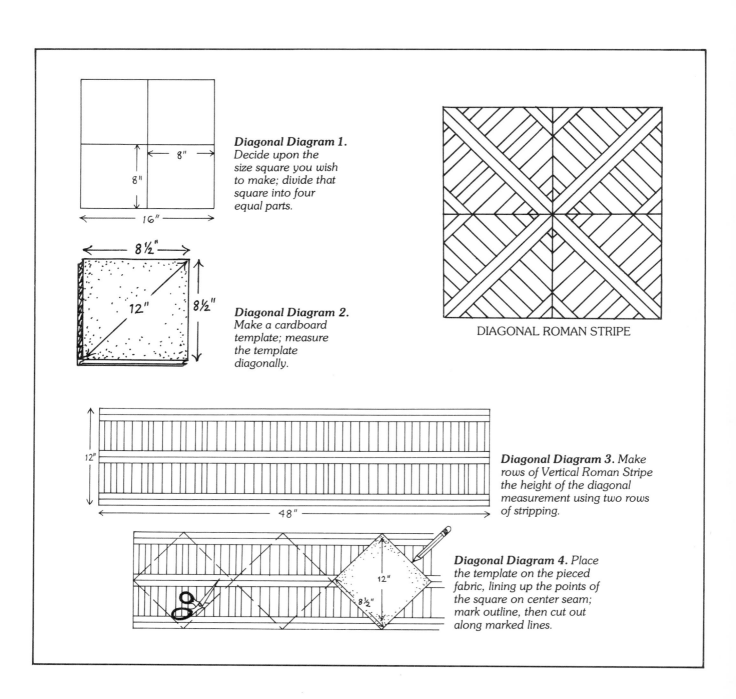

Diagonal Diagram 1. *Decide upon the size square you wish to make; divide that square into four equal parts.*

Diagonal Diagram 2. *Make a cardboard template; measure the template diagonally.*

DIAGONAL ROMAN STRIPE

Diagonal Diagram 3. *Make rows of Vertical Roman Stripe the height of the diagonal measurement using two rows of stripping.*

Diagonal Diagram 4. *Place the template on the pieced fabric, lining up the points of the square on center seam; mark outline, then cut out along marked lines.*

Diagonal Roman Stripe Variation

Make string material, then cut into narrow strips as shown in *Variation Diagram 1*. Cut a fabric or paper base to the block size you wish to make. Sew the pieced material diagonally across base, trimming the ends even with the base *(Variation Diagram 2)*. With right sides facing and raw edges even, sew a strip of fabric to one side of the pieced center making a ¼″ seam *(Variation Diagram 3)*. Turn and press to right side, then continue adding strips of even width to each side of pieced center until entire block is covered *(Variation Diagram 4)*. To achieve the straight edges seen in Diagram 4, turn block over and trim away excess material even with edges of base (see *Figure 27* on page 10). Make at least four squares and join as shown in the illustration.

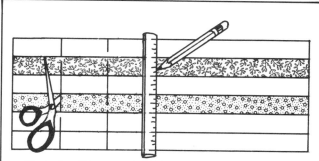

Variation Diagram 1. Make string material, then cut into narrow even strips.

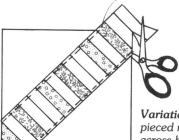

Variation Diagram 2. Sew pieced material diagonally across base; trim ends even with base.

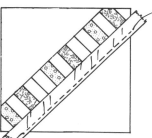

Variation Diagram 3. Sew fabric strip to one side of pieced center with right sides facing and raw edges even, making a ¼″ seam. **Variation Diagram 4.** Continue adding strips until entire base is covered.

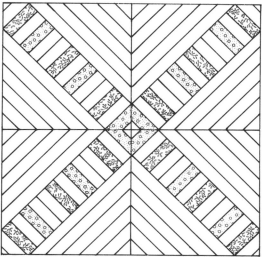

DIAGONAL ROMAN STRIPE VARIATION

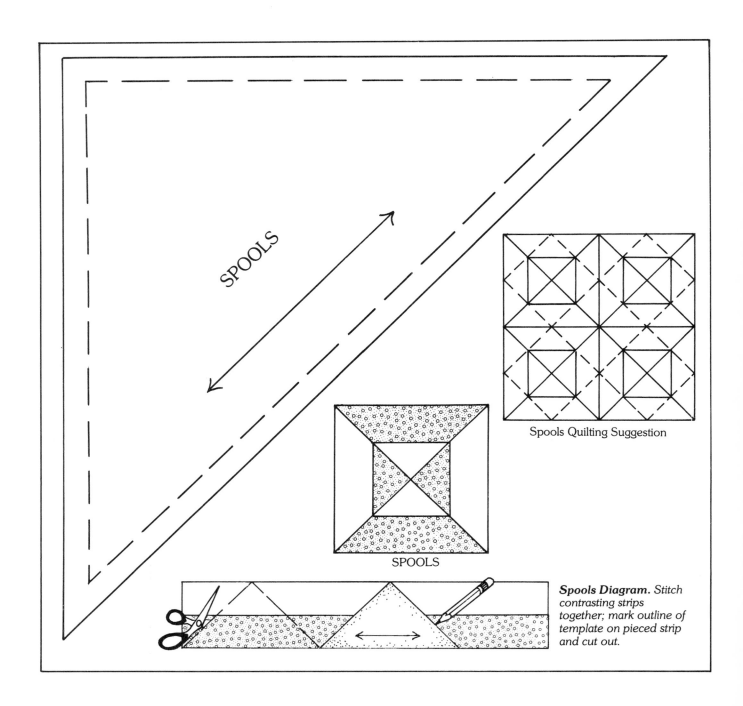

SPOOLS

Spools Quilting Suggestion

SPOOLS

Spools Diagram. Stitch contrasting strips together; mark outline of template on pieced strip and cut out.

STRIP PIECING TO FORM TRIANGLE DESIGNS

Strip piecing can add a new dimension to traditional triangle patchwork designs. Become adept at strip-pieced triangle patchwork by making the designs given here, then use your new skills to adapt your favorite triangle designs to this method.

Spools

Block Size: 7¾″ square.

This simple but striking design is made by cutting two contrasting strips of fabric, each 2½″ wide. Sew the strips together and press the seam allowances to one side; the pieced strips will measure 4½″ in width. Following the directions on page 4—Template Supplies, make a *Spools* template using the pattern given above. Position the template on the pieced strip and trace around the edge to transfer the outline to the fabric; cut out as shown in the *Spools Diagram*. Rearrange the triangles to form the spool design. Sew the triangles together in halves (lower left and upper right), then sew the halves together, matching the seams carefully. You might want to try the quilting suggestion illustrated above.

Twilight

Block Size: 9¼″ square.

Two pieced strips of contrasting fabric are needed to create this design. Cut four strips, each 4″ wide, and sew together making two 7½″-wide pieced strips. Press the seam allowances to one side. Following the directions on page 4—Template Supplies, make a *Twilight* template using the pattern on page 24.

Following *Twilight Diagram 1*, position the template,

right side up, on the strip; mark triangles along the entire length as shown. Following *Twilight Diagram 2*, turn the template over and mark triangles across the second strip; these triangles will be opposite to the first group. Cut out the triangles, then piece together, making four squares (*Twilight Diagram 3*). Sew the squares together, making two halves, then sew the halves together forming the *Twilight* design; be sure to match all seams carefully. Refer to the illustration below for an excellent quilting suggestion.

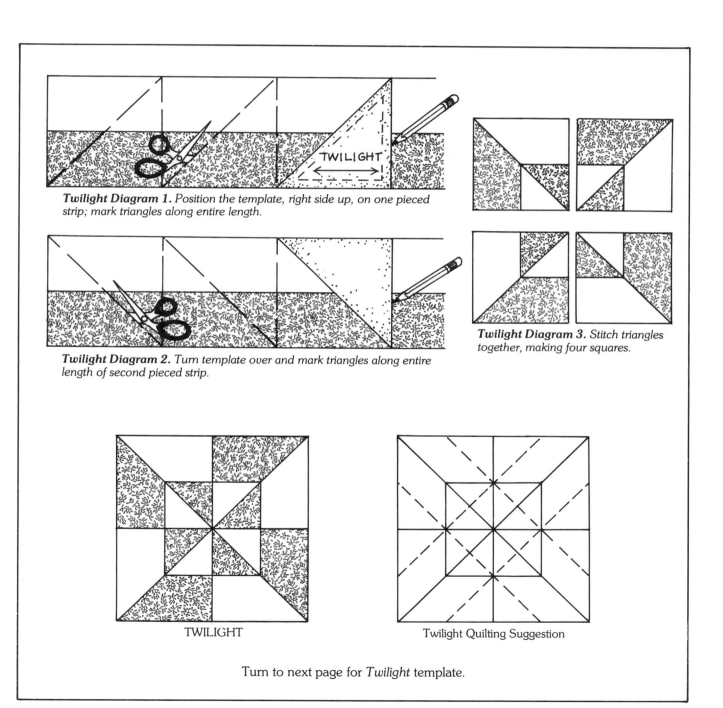

Twilight Diagram 1. *Position the template, right side up, on one pieced strip; mark triangles along entire length.*

Twilight Diagram 2. *Turn template over and mark triangles along entire length of second pieced strip.*

Twilight Diagram 3. *Stitch triangles together, making four squares.*

TWILIGHT

Twilight Quilting Suggestion

Turn to next page for *Twilight* template.

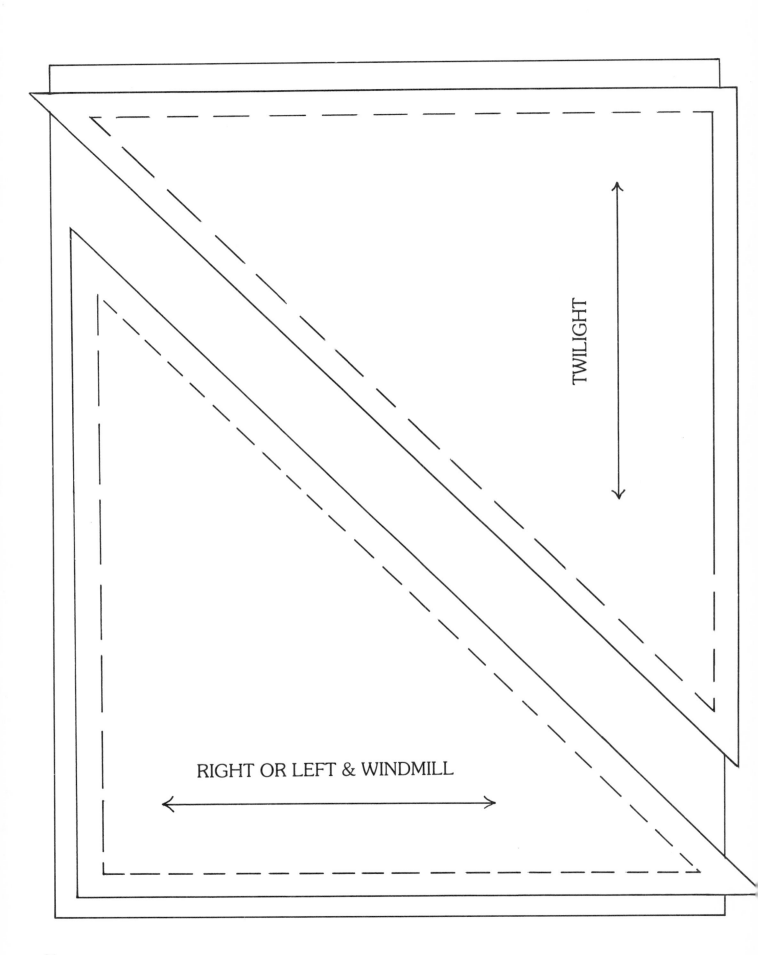

TWILIGHT

RIGHT OR LEFT & WINDMILL

Right or Left

Block Size: 9″ square.

Cut two strips of contrasting fabric, each 3⅞″ wide; sew together, making one 7¼″-wide pieced strip. Press the seam allowances to one side. Following the directions on page 4—Template Supplies, make a *Right or Left* template using the pattern given on the facing page. Position the template on the pieced strip and trace around the edge to transfer the outline to the fabric (see *Right or Left Diagram*); cut out along marked lines. Arrange the triangles to form one of the two examples illustrated; sew triangles together in halves, then sew the halves together.

Use stripping between all blocks when setting them together for a quilt top; some blocks will swirl in one direction, and others in another direction. A simple quilting design is shown here.

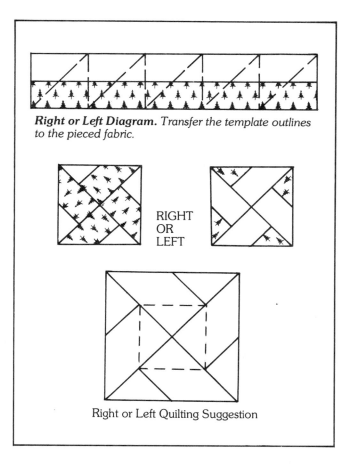

Right or Left Diagram. *Transfer the template outlines to the pieced fabric.*

RIGHT OR LEFT

Right or Left Quilting Suggestion

Windmill

Block Size: 9″ square.

This design is a variation of *Right or Left,* and illustrates how the same design can be changed radically by varying the number of strips. To make *Windmill,* cut three strips of contrasting but harmonizing fabric, each 2¾″ wide. Sew the three strips together, making one 7¼″-wide strip; press the seam allowances to one side. Following the directions on page 4—Template Supplies, make a *Windmill* template using the pattern given on the facing page. Position the template on the pieced strip and trace around the edge; cut out along marked lines. Arrange the triangles to form one of the two examples illustrated; sew triangles together in halves, then sew the halves together.

Use stripping between all blocks when setting them together for a quilt top; some blocks will swirl in one direction, and others in another direction. Refer to the quilting suggestion for an exciting design which is sure to add motion to your quilt.

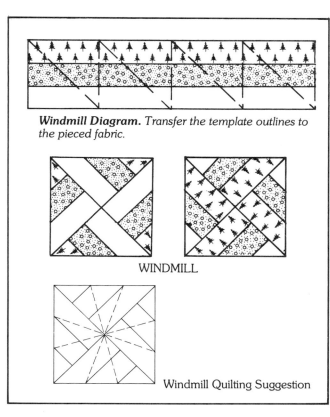

Windmill Diagram. *Transfer the template outlines to the pieced fabric.*

WINDMILL

Windmill Quilting Suggestion

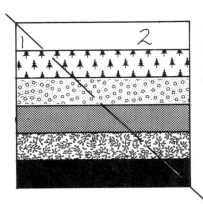

Deco Diagram 1.
Rule diagonally across the first group of 24 squares.

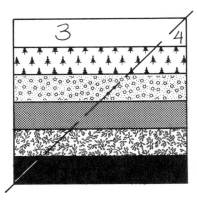

Deco Diagram 2.
Rule diagonally in the opposite direction for the remaining 24 squares.

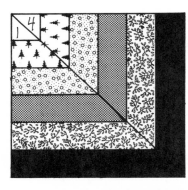

Deco Diagram 3.
Square A: Sew triangles 1 and 4 together.

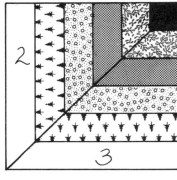

Square B: Sew triangles 2 and 3 together.

Deco Echo

Block Size: 12″ square.

This unusual but simple design is especially striking when worked up in colors that seem to "echo" one another; I used several shades of pink to create the design in the photograph.

To make a 72″ × 96″ quilt, 12 complete blocks will be needed; each complete block is composed of four 12″ squares; set three blocks across and four down. Use six different fabrics in harmonizing colors: two or three solids and several small prints, checks or stripes will work well. For a 45″-wide fabric, buy 1⅛ yards each of six different fabrics; lining fabric will also be necessary.

Press fabrics, then position on flat surface and mark off 2½″-wide strips using a yardstick; see *Figure 2* on page 6. Cut out strips carefully along marked lines; cut off all selvages. Determine the arrangement of the color bands, then sew strips together in groups of six, making 16 pieced groups, *all exactly alike*. Press seam allowances to one side. Following *Figure 37* on page 14, square-off pieced strips and mark cutting lines; each square should measure 12½″ × 12½″ (check continually for accuracy when squaring-off and cutting). Three squares of this size can be cut from each of the 16 strips, making 48 squares in total.

Divide the squares into two groups of 24. Using a yardstick, rule diagonally across the first group of 24 squares following *Deco Diagram 1;* cut out, forming 48 triangles. Using tailor's chalk, number the triangles as shown, then stack into two groups by number. Following *Deco Diagram 2,* rule diagonally across the remaining 24

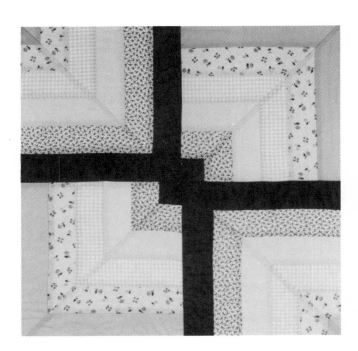

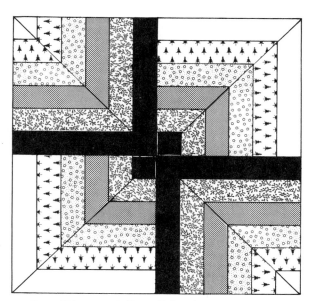

Deco Diagram 4. *Deco Echo Assembly Diagram (pictured in photograph).*

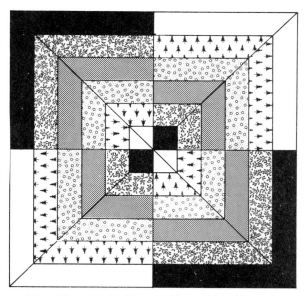

Deco Diagram 5. *Alternate Deco Echo Assembly Diagram.*

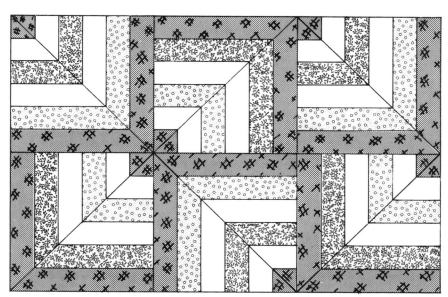

Deco Diagram 6. *For an alternate effect, use five fabrics, sewing the same fabric along each outside edge.*

squares in the direction *opposite* the first 24; cut out as shown and mark numbers on each half using tailor's chalk. Stack into two groups by number. Assemble the triangles following *Deco Diagram 3,* sewing triangles 1 and 4 together for square A, and sewing triangles 2 and 3 together for square B. Assemble the squares following *Deco Diagrams 4* or *5.*

For an alternate effect that resembles bordered blocks, use five fabrics instead of six, buying 2¼ yards of a darker harmonizing color of one of the five fabrics. Cut out strips as described above, and assemble six rows of strips with the same dark fabric along each outside edge. Stitch, cut and assemble as described above. The finished effect will resemble *Deco Diagram 6.*

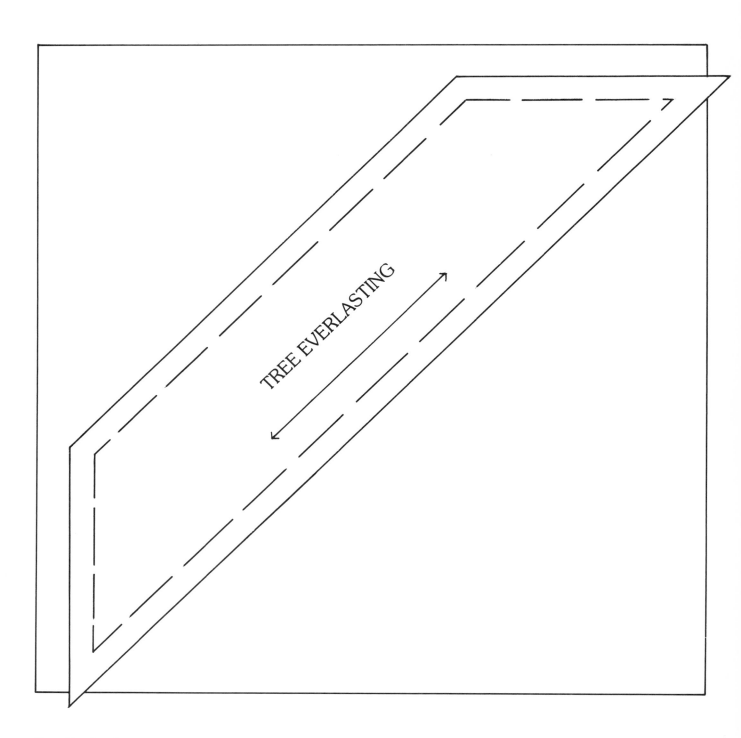

TREE EVERLASTING

Tree Everlasting

Only one pattern piece is needed to create all the pretty designs shown on the next page. The position of the pieces and the dramatic color changes from light to dark make this design appear more complicated than it really is. Choose two colors of fabric or make a scrap quilt using prints and solids, making sure there is a great contrast between light and dark.

Following the directions on page 4—Template Supplies, make a *Tree Everlasting* template using the pattern

given above. Mark and cut 2"-wide strips of fabric following *Figure 2* on page 6. Referring to *Tree Diagram 1*, mark and cut out patchwork pieces using the template. Following one of the color arrangements given on the next page or your own original design, sew the bias edges of the patchwork pieces together as shown in *Tree Diagram 2*, making long pieced strips. Continue adding pieces until each strip measures the desired width of the project. Sew the strips together, matching or centering seams carefully as shown in the diagrams.

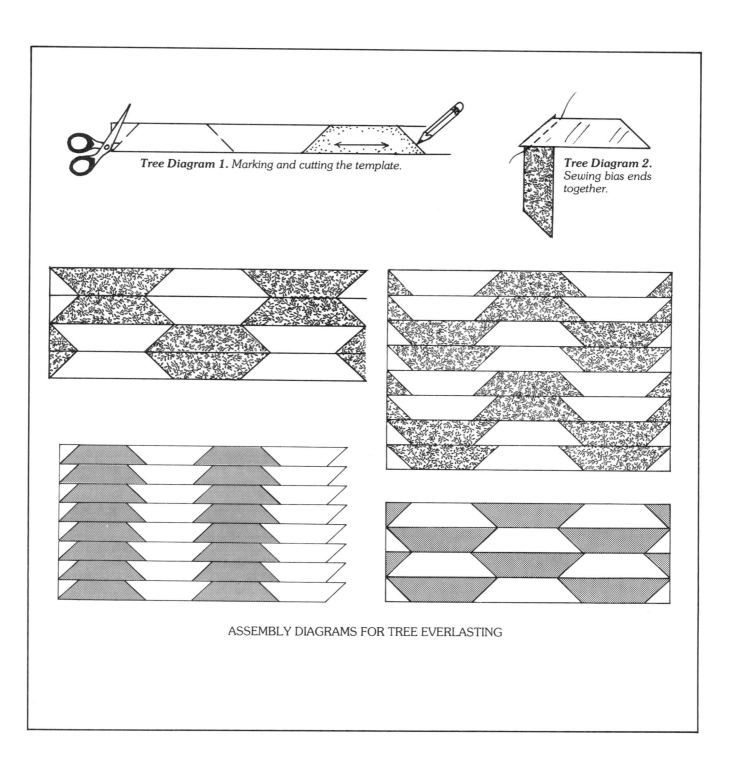

Tree Diagram 1. Marking and cutting the template.

Tree Diagram 2. Sewing bias ends together.

ASSEMBLY DIAGRAMS FOR TREE EVERLASTING

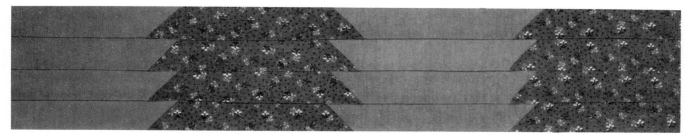

CHAPTER 2

Strip Piecing to Form Log Cabin Designs

The popular *Log Cabin* design has innumerable variations. The traditional form of the design, shown in the border and on the next page, uses contrasting rectangular strips of light and dark pieces in a regular pattern. Each block is built around a central square, with the narrow strips surrounding the center; these strips represent the overlapping logs used to build the cabins of the early settlers. Many of the old *Log Cabin* quilts can be found with a red center square simulating the chimney or hearth of the cabin. The placement of light and dark strips of fabric simulates the effect of sunlight and shadow on the cabin. Traditionally, no border is used on this quilt.

Variations of the *Log Cabin* pattern can be brought about in many ways. When assembling a *quilt* of traditional blocks, the placement of the light and dark sides of the blocks can be altered; some variations are illustrated on page 33. When assembling a *block*, the placement of the light and dark strips can vary, the width of the strips can vary, the position of the center square can be moved, or the center square itself can be changed into another shape such as a triangle or rectangle. The way the strips are placed around the center also adds considerable variation to this design. Many *Log Cabin* modifications will be covered in this chapter; all of these are suitable for the quilt-as-you-go method, although the stitching must always end $\frac{1}{4}''$–$\frac{1}{2}''$ away from all edges to facilitate attachment of the blocks.

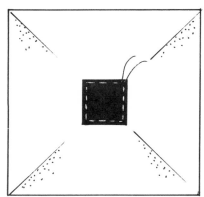

Figure 39. Pin the center piece in exact center of the base; machine-baste in place ⅛" from raw edges.

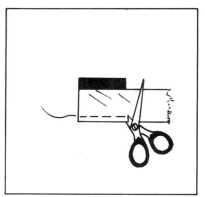

Figure 40. Pin the first light strip of fabric in place; stitch ¼" from edges, then trim away the excess fabric.

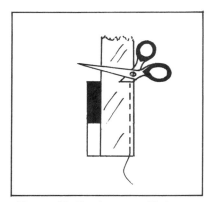

Figure 41. Pin the second light strip of fabric in place; stitch ¼" from edges, then trim away the excess fabric.

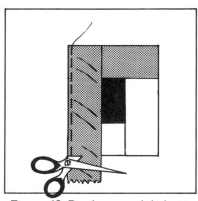

Figure 42. Pin the second dark strip of fabric in place; stitch ¼" from edges, then trim away excess fabric.

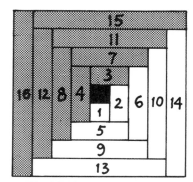

TRADITIONAL LOG CABIN

GENERAL DIRECTIONS

When choosing fabrics, select either prints or solids or a combination of both with as much contrast as possible between the light and dark shades. Sort all fabrics into a light pile and a dark pile; discard any fabrics that do not show great contrast. Woolens, velvets, silks and satins, even ribbons of various kinds have been used successfully to make *Log Cabin* designs; cottons, primarily calico prints and solid chintzes, have been used to make the *Log Cabin* samples shown in color on the inside covers of this book.

Following is a sew-and-cut method of assembling the *Traditional Log Cabin* design on a base. The length of each strip will be determined after each strip is sewn to the base. Machine-sewing is recommended.

(1) For the base, cut a paper or muslin square to the desired size; fold on the diagonal both ways to determine the exact center of the square. (Individual directions are given for finding the center of a triangle or rectangle design where applicable.)

(2) Cut light and dark fabrics into strips of equal width (the traditional width is 1½", which includes a ¼" seam allowance at each edge).

(3) Cut a center piece 1½" square (or use a template to cut a triangle or other shape) from red or another color fabric.

(4) Pin the center piece (square, triangle, etc.), right side up, in exact center of the fabric or paper base; machine-baste in place ⅛" from raw edges *(Figure 39)*. **Note:** If assembling block by the quilt-as-you-go method, hand-baste center piece in place; do not machine-baste.

(5) With right sides facing, pin the first light strip of fabric to the center piece; stitch together ¼″ from edges, then trim away the excess fabric, even with the edge of the center piece *(Figure 40);* press strip to the right side.

(6) Pin a second light strip to the center piece and first strip; stitch in place, making a ¼″ seam, and trim away excess fabric *(Figure 41);* press the second light strip to the right side.

(7) Pin the first dark strip to the center and second light strip; stitch in place and trim away excess fabric. Press the first dark strip to the right side.

(8) Pin the second dark strip to the center and first dark strip; stitch in place and trim away excess fabric *(Figure 42);* press to the right side. This completes the first round of strips.

Continue in this manner, adding light strips to two sides of the center, and dark strips to the other two sides. This will divide the light and dark areas on the diagonal through the center of the block. Although there are variations in color and placement of strips throughout this chapter, the same rules of pinning, stitching, trimming

and pressing the strips apply to all of the *Log Cabin* designs. **Note:** Be sure to *finger*-press strips in place if using the quilt-as-you-go method. The directions for most of the following designs will refer back to this section, so become thoroughly familiar with Steps 1–8 before beginning any *Log Cabin* design.

ASSEMBLING A TRADITIONAL LOG CABIN QUILT

Following are some illustrations of the various ways in which traditional *Log Cabin* quilt blocks can be assembled. To emphasize the shading of the blocks, the center red square has been eliminated from the illustrations and the blocks have been divided into triangles of light and dark.

The variations are as interesting as they are endless. My suggestion would be to arrange your finished blocks on a large flat surface in several of the ways illustrated here or in some of your own arrangements. Determine which design appeals to you most, then assemble the blocks in that way.

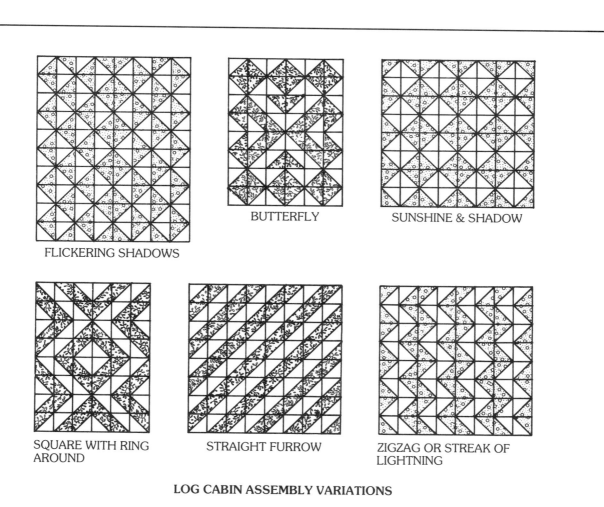

FLICKERING SHADOWS

BUTTERFLY

SUNSHINE & SHADOW

SQUARE WITH RING AROUND

STRAIGHT FURROW

ZIGZAG OR STREAK OF LIGHTNING

LOG CABIN ASSEMBLY VARIATIONS

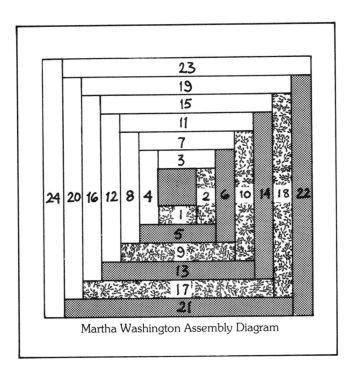

Martha Washington Assembly Diagram

Martha Washington's Log Cabin

Shown in color on the inside front cover.
Block Size: 15″ square.

This is a modification of the traditional *Log Cabin*. The design varies from the traditional in three ways: the center square is larger, the light strips are a solid color, and the dark side of the square alternates with solid medium and printed fabric strips.

Use a pretty print with tiny motifs; select one color to combine with the print for the alternating bands of color on the dark side of the square (see photograph). The other half of the square should be made from a lighter shade of the solid you have chosen, or from white fabric or muslin.

Cut a 15½″ × 15½″ square of paper or fabric for the base. Cut the center square, 3½″ × 3½″, from the solid medium fabric. Cut all fabric strips 1½″ wide from light solid, medium solid and print fabric. Following the diagram for placement of light, medium and printed fabrics, assemble the block as directed in Steps 1–8 on pages 32–33.

English Log Cabin or Courthouse Steps

Block Size: 9″ square.

Another *Log Cabin* variation, this design features three squares in the center. Light and dark colors are positioned on opposite sides of the block, and the strips are joined to the center on opposite sides rather than in rounds.

Choose different prints in two distinct shades or a light solid and a dark print as shown in the illustration. Washed, unbleached muslin handles beautifully and could be used for the light color, combined with an attractive print with a tiny motif for the dark color.

Cut a 9½″ × 9½″ square of paper or fabric for the base. Cut the center square, 1½″ × 1½″, from the light fabric. Cut two squares, 1½″ × 1½″, from the dark fabric for the first strips. Cut all fabric strips 1½″ wide from light and dark fabric. Following the diagram for placement of light and dark fabric and for the position of the strips, assemble the block as directed in Steps 1–8 on pages 32–33. Remember that this design varies from the traditional *Log Cabin* in the placement of the strips, so add the strips to *opposite* sides of the center as shown in the *English Diagram*.

The *Assembly Diagram for English Log Cabin* shows an interesting arrangement of *English Log Cabin* blocks. Cut solid 9½″ squares from the light and dark fabrics, and alternate those squares with the pieced squares to create a sawtooth design. This arrangement is a quick and easy way to make a quilt because you will only have to make half the number of pieced blocks!

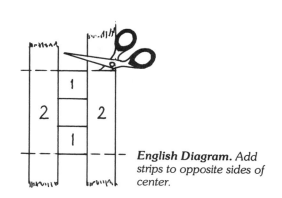

English Diagram. Add strips to opposite sides of center.

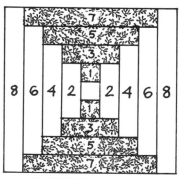

ENGLISH LOG CABIN

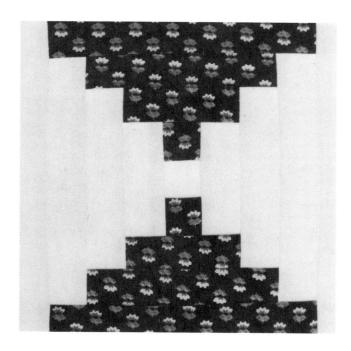

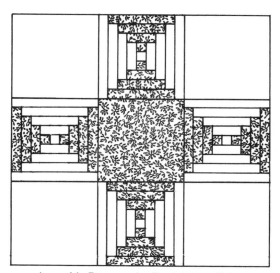

Assembly Diagram for English Log Cabin

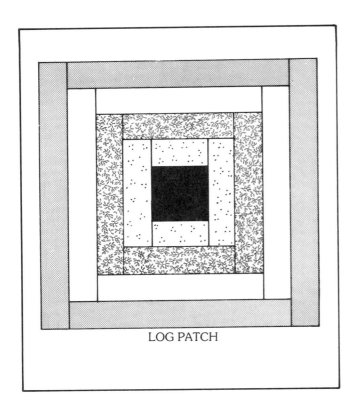

LOG PATCH

Log Patch

Shown in color on the inside back cover.
Block Size: 10″ square.

The construction of this block is identical to the *English Log Cabin,* except for the placement of the light and dark strips and the size of the center square (which is larger). Notice that the block has concentric bands of color, all cut the same width, which encircle the center square. The same design constructed with light and dark strips on *opposite* sides of the center square becomes the design called *White House Steps;* see the photograph below right.

When constructing *Log Patch,* choose light and dark fabrics with great contrast for the alternating bands of color. If using a different fabric for each round, make the center square red for a traditional effect.

Cut 10½″ × 10½″ square of paper or fabric for the base. Cut center square, 2½″ × 2½″, from light or red fabric. Cut all fabric strips 1½″ wide. Following the illustration for placement of colors and position of strips, assemble the block as directed in Steps 1–8 on pages 32–33; strips are added to opposite sides of center as shown in the *English Diagram* on page 35.

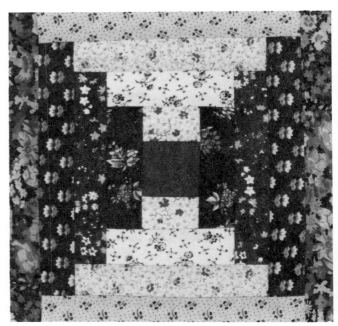

WHITE HOUSE STEPS

Echo Log Cabin

Block Size: 6″ square.

This design is an easy variation of *Log Cabin* that begins with a square in the corner. Strips of alternating colors and prints are added on two sides.

Use red for the corner square; select pretty prints or dramatic solids of contrasting light and dark fabrics for the strips. If using stripping to connect the finished squares, use red (or the same color used for the corner square).

Cut a 6½″ × 6½″ square of paper or fabric for the base. Cut the corner square, 2½″ × 2½″, from red or desired color fabric. Cut all fabric strips 1½″ wide. Following *Echo Diagram 1*, position the red square right side up in one corner; stitch in place ⅛″ from edges. With right sides facing, add first strip to square and stitch in place; trim away excess as shown in *Echo Diagram 2*, then press strip to the right side. Following *Echo Diagram 3*, stitch the second strip to the corner square and first strip, trim away excess, then turn to the right side. Continue in this manner for the rest of the block, using the same color or print for each row as shown in the illustration, or using random colors and prints as shown in the photograph below.

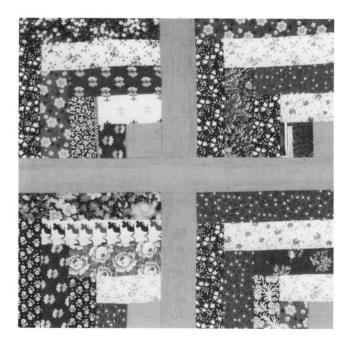

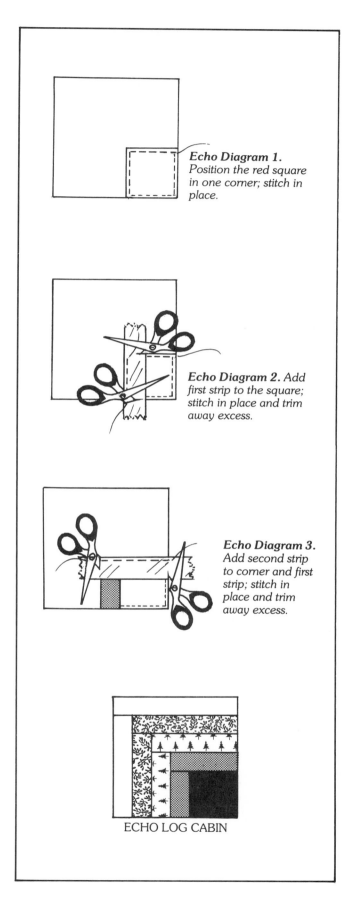

Echo Diagram 1. Position the red square in one corner; stitch in place.

Echo Diagram 2. Add first strip to the square; stitch in place and trim away excess.

Echo Diagram 3. Add second strip to corner and first strip; stitch in place and trim away excess.

ECHO LOG CABIN

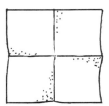 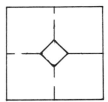

Hung Diagram 1. Fold base in half on the straight to find center. ***Hung Diagram 2.*** Place each corner of center square on one of the folds and stitch in place.

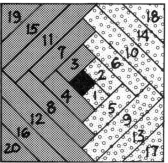

HUNG CENTER LOG CABIN

Hung Center Log Cabin

Block Size: 9″ square.

A unique version of the *Log Cabin,* this design has a "hung" center square, that is, a square which has been turned, forming a diamond. The block is shaded in the traditional manner, but what a difference a turn makes!

Select fabrics with tiny motifs that show a great contrast between light and dark. Solids and prints can be combined, providing that they are within the same shade of light or dark. The center square should be red or another dominant color which is repeated throughout the quilt.

Cut a 9½″ × 9½″ square of paper or fabric for the base. Fold in half on the straight to find the center and indicate placement of the center square *(Hung Diagram 1).* Cut the center square, 2½″ × 2½″, from the red or dominant fabric and place each corner of the square on one of the folds as shown in *Hung Diagram 2;* stitch in place ⅛″ from the edges. Cut all fabric strips 1½″ wide. Following the diagram for placement of light and dark fabric and position of the strips, assemble the block as directed in Steps 1–8 on pages 32–33. This block can be made any size; simply keep adding strips around the center until the base is covered.

Off-Center Log Cabin

Shown in color on the inside back cover.
Block Size: 9″ square.

The versatile *Log Cabin* takes on a different appearance with yet another variation: an off-center square and strips of two widths. Note that this arrangement creates the impression of a curved line between the light and dark areas; this effect suggests many exciting and innovative block combinations based on the curved line.

Experiment with solid shades of two colors for the light and dark sides (see the color photograph for an example). Choose six shades of a solid light color and six shades of a solid dark color plus a neutral shade for the center. There should be good contrast between the light and the dark.

Cut a 9½″ × 9½″ square of paper or fabric for the base. Cut the center square, 1½″ × 1½″, from the neutral shade of fabric. Cut all light fabrics into strips 1½″ wide; cut all the dark fabrics into strips 1″ wide. Measure 3¼″ in from the lower right corner of the base as shown in *Off-Center Diagram* and draw intersecting lines. Pin the center square to the base as shown and stitch in place, ⅛″ from the edges. Following the photograph for placement of light and dark fabrics, assemble the block as directed in Steps 1–8 on pages 32–33.

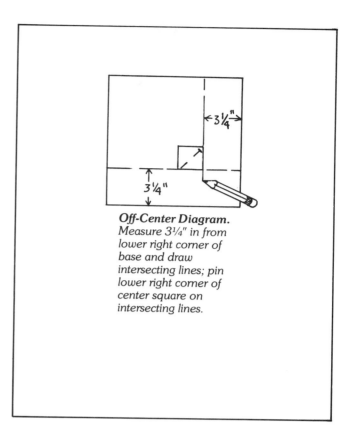

Off-Center Diagram.
Measure 3¼″ in from lower right corner of base and draw intersecting lines; pin lower right corner of center square on intersecting lines.

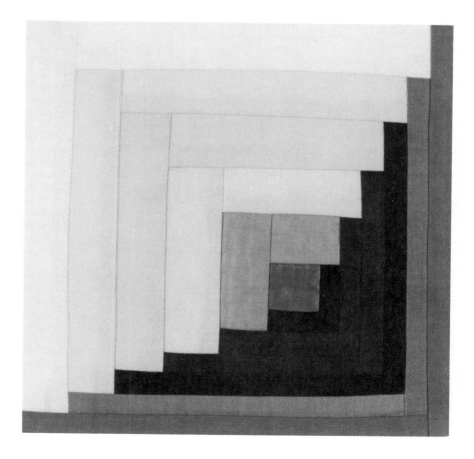

Marching Squares

Shown in color on the inside back cover.
Block Size: 10″ square.

This is an excellent example of how the sew-and-cut method (see page 13) can create a patchwork block that appears difficult, but is really quick and simple to do. The center square actually consists of four smaller squares, easily pieced together. One half of the "logs" in the block are pieced strips.

Select any two highly contrasting fabrics, solids or prints, to make a pretty design. Solid red and muslin were used in the sample that appears in the color photograph.

Cut a 10½″ × 10½″ square of paper or fabric for the base. For the pieced center squares, cut a strip 1¾″ high and the width of the fabric from the light fabric and the dark fabric. Sew the strips together, right sides facing, making a ¼″ seam; press seam allowance toward the dark fabric. Following *Marching Diagram 1*, measure, mark and cut strips from the pieced fabric, each 1¾″ wide. To assemble the center square, sew two pieced strips together, alternating the position of the small light and dark squares as shown in the photograph. For the logs, cut a strip from the dark fabric, 1¾″ high and the

width of the fabric. Cut a strip of muslin, 10″ high and the width of the muslin. Sew the red strip to one long edge of the muslin, right sides facing and raw edges even, making a ¼″ seam; press the seam allowance toward the dark fabric. Following *Marching Diagram 2*, measure, mark and cut 1¾″-high strips from the pieced fabric. One half of the block is composed of plain muslin strips; cut several 1¾″-high strips from muslin, the width of the muslin.

To assemble the block, find the center of the base by folding twice, then stitch the pieced square in exact center. Using the sew-and-cut method of assembly (see page 13), stitch log #1 in place using a plain muslin strip and cutting away excess muslin even with center square as shown in *Marching Diagram 3*. Stitch a plain strip to left side of center for log #2. Following *Marching Diagram 4*, stitch first pieced strip (log #3) in place, positioning dark square at left and matching seam of square with seam from log #2; cut away excess muslin as shown. Stitch log #4 to right side of center, using a pieced strip and following *Marching Diagram 5*. Continue in this counterclockwise manner, sewing plain strips to top and left sides of center, and pieced strips to bottom and right sides of center. Check that seams match perfectly on each round.

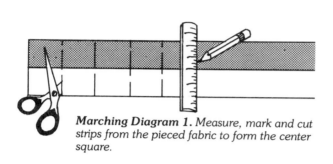

Marching Diagram 1. *Measure, mark and cut strips from the pieced fabric to form the center square.*

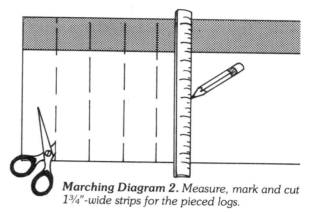

Marching Diagram 2. *Measure, mark and cut 1¾"-wide strips for the pieced logs.*

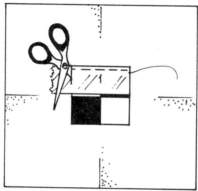

Marching Diagram 3. *Stitch log #1 in place: trim away excess.*

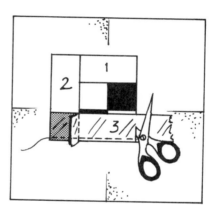

Marching Diagram 4. *Stitch first pieced log in place; position dark square at left.*

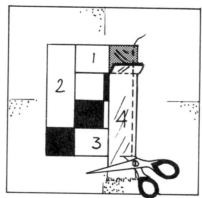

Marching Diagram 5. *Stitch pieced log #4 to right side of center; trim away excess.*

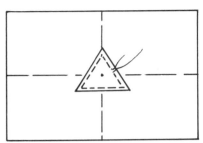

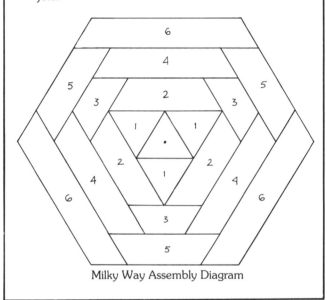

Milky Way Diagram. *Place dot of triangle on exact center of base; position tip of triangle on the fold.*

Milky Way Assembly Diagram

Milky Way

Shown in color on the inside back cover.
Block Size: Approximately 10¼″ × 12″.

This lovely old pattern dating from the 1800's is an interesting version of *Log Cabin*. It is constructed using templates rather than the sew-and-cut method because accuracy is extremely important when setting the blocks together. Following the directions on page 4 — Template Supplies, make templates 1–6 using the patterns given on the next page.

Select two highly contrasting fabrics such as the solid and print I used in my sample block (see the color photograph).

Cut a 10¾″ × 12½″ piece of paper or fabric for the base. Fold in half on the straight to find the center and indicate placement of the center triangle. Using template 1, cut the center triangle from the dark fabric; indicate position of dot on fabric with a pin. Place the triangle on the base so the dot is on the exact center point and the tip of the triangle is on the fold as shown in the *Milky Way Diagram*; stitch in place ⅛″ from raw edges. Use template 1 to cut three triangles from light fabric. Cut light and dark fabric into strips 1¾″ wide. Use templates 2, 4 and 6 to cut three pieces each from dark fabric strips; use templates 3 and 5 to cut three pieces each from light fabric strips. **Note:** See *Tree Diagram 1* on page 29 for a "quick-cut" method for cutting these templates.

With right sides facing and raw edges even, stitch each of the three triangles to center making a ¼″ seam; turn and press each triangle to the right side, forming a larger triangle. Next, stitch long edges of the three #2 pieces to each side of the large triangle; turn and press to the right side forming a hexagon. Continue adding strips around center in numerical order following the diagram for placement, and turning and pressing each strip to the right side after stitching.

When block is complete, trim fabric base even with the edges of the block or gently tear away the paper base. The finished block should be a perfect hexagon, measuring 6½″ on each side. When joining the hexagons, match the dark edges for a pretty allover design.

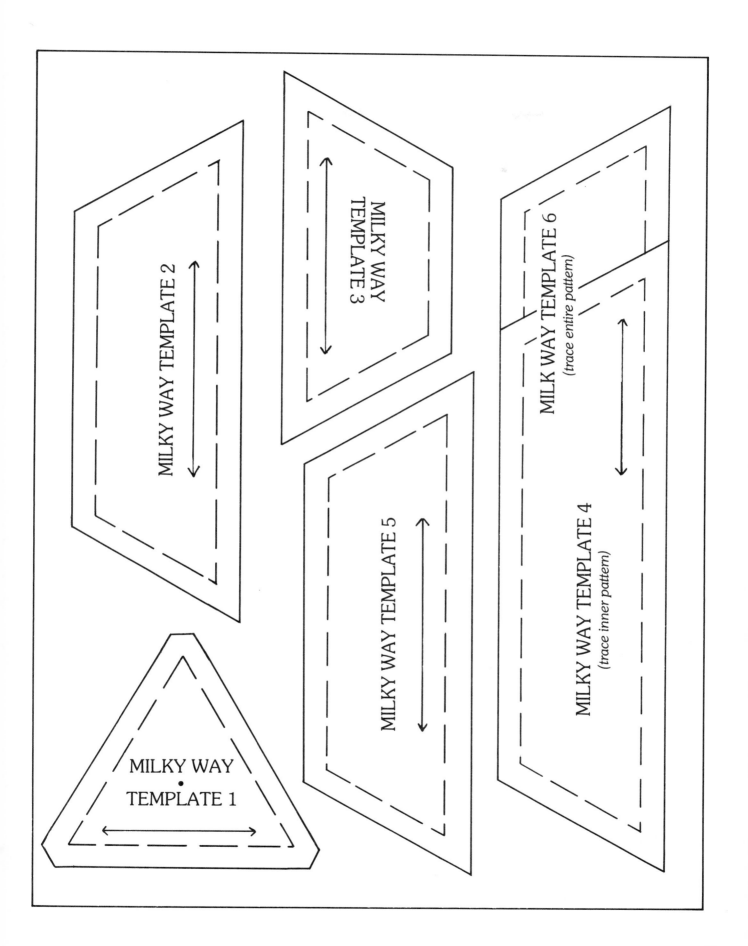

MILKY WAY TEMPLATE 2

MILKY WAY TEMPLATE 3

MILK WAY TEMPLATE 6
(trace entire pattern)

MILKY WAY TEMPLATE 5

MILKY WAY TEMPLATE 4
(trace inner pattern)

MILKY WAY
TEMPLATE 1

Pyramid Log Cabin

Design by Fred Calland, Arlington, Virginia.
Shown in color on the inside back cover.
Block Size: Approximately 10½" high × 12" wide.

The *Pyramid Log Cabin* is an original, non-traditional design which utilizes the same basic *Log Cabin* techniques for assembly already given in this chapter. Templates are given for this design, although the sew-and-cut method can also be used; you must use a template for the center triangle. Following the directions on page 4—Template Supplies, make a template for the center triangle and for pieces 1–9 using the patterns given here.

Select four different fabrics for a pretty effect; use light, medium and dark fabric for each of the three sides and a contrasting fabric for the center. See the photograph on the inside back cover for one color suggestion.

Cut an 11" × 12½" piece of paper or fabric for the base. Fold in half on the straight to find the center and indicate placement of the center triangle. Using the triangle template, cut one triangle from desired fabric; indicate position of dot on fabric with a pin. Place the triangle on the base so the dot is on the exact center point and the tip of the triangle is on the fold; see *Milky Way Diagram* on page 42. Following the photograph for placement of fabric strips, use templates 1, 4 and 7 to cut one piece each from a medium solid; cut print strips using templates 2, 5 and 8; cut dark solid strips using templates 3, 6 and 9. **Note:** See *Tree Diagram 1* on page 29 for a "quick-cut" method for cutting these templates.

With right sides facing and raw edges even, stitch the fabric strips around the center triangle in numerical order; make ¼" seams. Turn and press each strip to the right side after stitching. When block is complete, trim fabric base even with the edges of the block or gently tear away the paper base. The finished block should be a perfect equilateral triangle, measuring 12½" on each side.

See *Pyramid Diagram 1* for a joining suggestion; *Pyramid Diagram 2* shows an entire quilt top joined in this manner. In order to create the straight edge, make template 10 following *Pyramid Diagram 3* and directions for making templates on page 4—Template Supplies; the measurements on the diagram include a ¼" seam allowance all around.

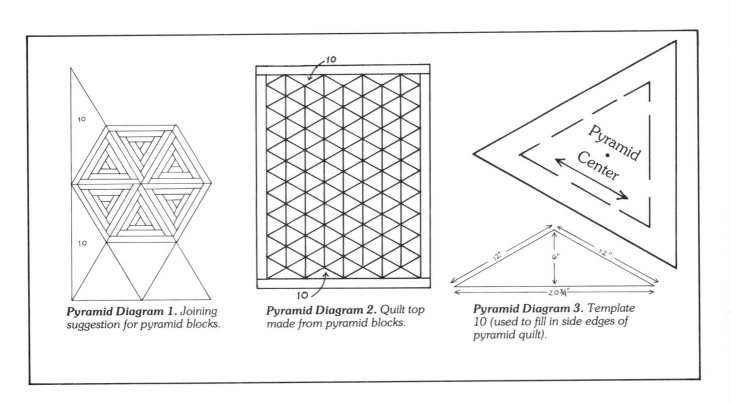

Pyramid Diagram 1. *Joining suggestion for pyramid blocks.*

Pyramid Diagram 2. *Quilt top made from pyramid blocks.*

Pyramid Diagram 3. *Template 10 (used to fill in side edges of pyramid quilt).*

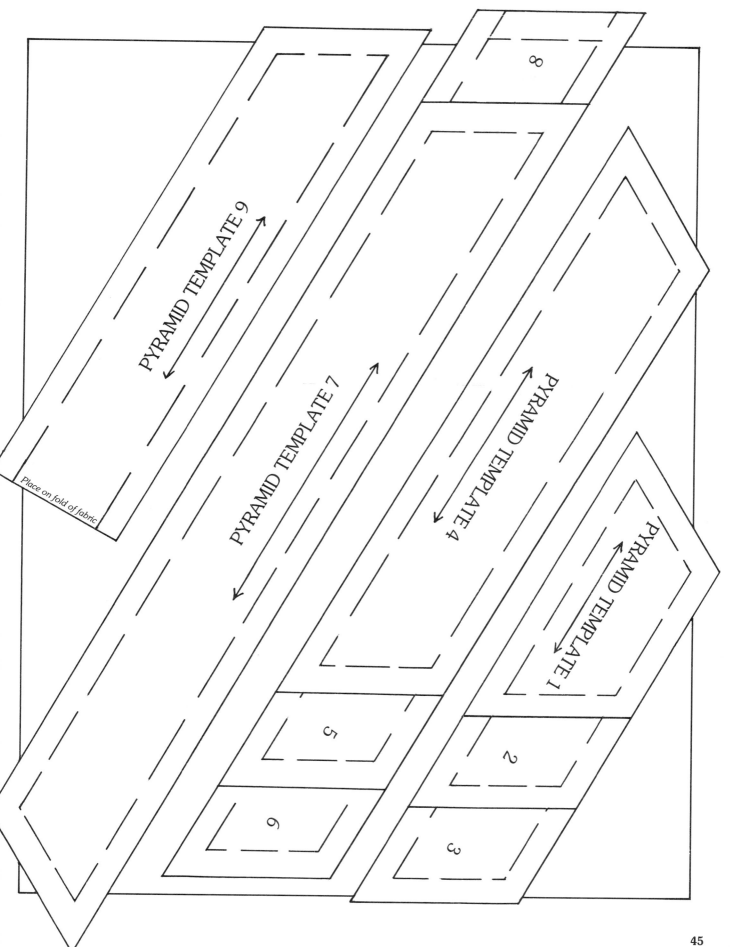

PYRAMID TEMPLATE 9

Place on fold of fabric

PYRAMID TEMPLATE 7

PYRAMID TEMPLATE 4

PYRAMID TEMPLATE 1

8

5

9

2

3

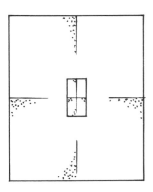

SKYSCRAPERS

Skyscraper Diagram. *Fold the rectangle in half on the straight to find the center; position on base matching fold lines.*

Skyscrapers

Block Size: 10″ × 12″.

This bold design has a rectangular center instead of the usual square of most *Log Cabins;* the block is therefore longer than it is wide. If made in bold solid colors, the design can be quite sophisticated, resembling the towers of a city skyline.

Select a solid bright color and white for this design. Use polished cotton for a modern effect; unbleached muslin can be substituted for the white for a similar effect. Red and white set with black stripping will create a striking quilt.

Cut a 10½″ × 12½″ piece of paper or fabric for the base. Fold in half on the straight to find the center and indicate placement of the center rectangle. Cut the center rectangle 2½″ × 4½″ from the white fabric; fold in half on the straight to find center, then position on base, matching fold lines as shown in the *Skyscraper Diagram.* Stitch in place ⅛″ from the edges. Cut all fabric strips 1½″ wide. Following the diagram for placement of dark and light and position of strips, assemble the block as directed in Steps 1–8 on pages 32–33.

CHAPTER 3
Making String Designs on a Shaped Base

Most traditional patchwork quilt designs are created by sewing shaped pieces together in a specified arrangement. Applying strings to a shaped base will add excitement, motion and color to an ordinary patchwork design. This chapter gives some examples of patchwork designs that are superbly suited to the application of strings. Read this chapter, study and experiment with the designs, then use your new skills to adapt your own favorite patchwork projects to string quilting!

All the templates in this section include a ¼″ seam allowance. Sew all pieces together with right sides facing and raw edges even, making ¼″ seams unless otherwise directed. Press all pieces to the right side after stitching them to the base. Where necessary, clip seam allowances at curves to keep the seams flat. Many of the designs are illustrated in black-and-white photographs with the directions; some color photographs are also given on the inside covers and the back cover.

OLD FASHIONED STRING QUILT

STRING DESIGNS ON A SQUARE BASE

Old-Fashioned String Quilt

This is one of the simplest string designs in this book. The square base can be any size, the strings can be any width or color, yet when four squares are joined together to form a block, interesting sub-designs will develop, depending upon the color placement and matching of the strings.

This is a scrap design meant to use up your extra fabric; however, a planned color scheme can be developed. When a predominant color, such as black, is used at the corners or diagonally across the center of the square, other squares are formed when the pieces are joined. If the strips are placed in the same position for all blocks, as in the sample drawn here, a border effect is obtained. Experiment with the placement of the predominant colors before assembling your quilt.

Cut a paper or fabric square, any size, for the base; this square must be the same size for all bases. The larger the base, the fewer blocks will be needed to complete the quilt; however, the fabric strips will have to be quite long in order to fit diagonally across each base. Cut fabrics, both prints and solids, in random widths. If using a predominant diagonal strip in your blocks, measure diagonally across the square and cut center strips of even width to the diagonal measurement.

Fold the base on the diagonal once for placement of the center strip. Center the first strip, right side up, on this fold and pin in place, letting the ends extend off the base. Stitch each long edge in place, making ⅛″ seams. With right sides facing, sew other strips to each side of the first strip, allowing the ends to extend off the base and making ¼″ seams. Fold and press each strip to the right side after stitching. Continue adding strips of various widths and colors to the base until the square is completed. If the last two rows at the corners are the same on all squares, a secondary design will be formed when the blocks are joined. Turn the square to the wrong side and trim away excess fabric, even with the edge of the base (see *Figure 27* on page 10). If paper was used for the base, gently tear it away at this time. When four squares are completed, stitch together, matching the predominant strips if applicable.

Amish Shadowed Square

The simplicity of this design, when assembled by the sew-and-cut method (see page 13), will allow you to create a beautiful quilt top in a few days instead of a few weeks. For an Amish look, use strong, solid colors for both strips and background. An exciting effect can be obtained by using harmonizing light colors for the strips, and black for the triangle. A pleasing yet simple quilt top can be created by applying the strips to the base in the same order for each block. A paper base must be used for this design.

Cut a paper square, any size, for the base; this square must be the same size for all bases. To make a template for the triangle, fold a square the size of the base in half on the diagonal; add ¼″ seam allowance to the diagonal edge, then cut away excess paper. Make a sturdy template using this triangle pattern and following directions on page 4 — Template Supplies. Use template to cut triangles from desired fabric; one triangle is needed for each block. Cut fabric strips to even widths of 1½″–2″.

With outer edges even, pin triangle, right side up, to base; stitch in place, ⅛″ from all edges. With right sides facing and raw edges even, pin edge of first strip to the diagonal edge of the triangle; stitch together, making ¼″ seam, then turn and press strip to the right side. With right sides facing, pin second strip to raw edge of first strip and stitch together in same manner. Continue adding strips until base is covered. Turn square to wrong side and trim away excess fabric, even with the edge of the base; see *Figure 27* on page 10. Gently tear away the paper base.

Experiment with the placement of the blocks before assembly. The traditional way to assemble this quilt is to place the string portion of each block in the same position.

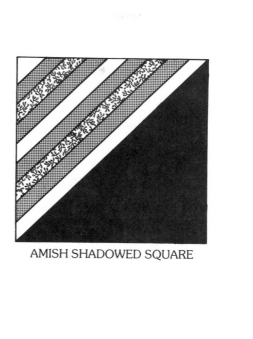

AMISH SHADOWED SQUARE

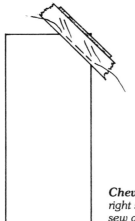

Chevron Diagram 1. *Pin a strip to the foundation at a 45° angle; sew each edge in place.*

Chevron Diagram 2. *With right sides facing, pin and sew a second strip to the first; after sewing, press the strip to the right side.*

Chevron Diagram 3. *Angle strips in opposite directions when sewing sections together.*

STRING DESIGN ON A STRIP BASE

Chevron

Chevron is constructed in lengthwise strips on a fabric or paper base. The length of the base is determined by the size of the project you are making; the width of the base should average 4″ for a quilt, 2″–3″ for a pillow or garment trim.

Cut the base strips to the desired length and width. Beginning at the upper corner of the base, pin a strip in place, right side up, at a 45° angle; see *Chevron Diagram 1.* Allow the ends of the fabric strip to extend beyond the edges of the fabric or paper, to be trimmed later. Sew each edge of the strip in place. Following *Chevron Diagram 2,* sew a second fabric strip to the lower edge of the first, with right sides facing, making a ¼″ seam and allowing the ends to extend beyond the base; turn to the right side and press. Continue adding random colors and widths of strips to the base. When the first section is completed, turn to the wrong side and trim the strip edges even with the base; see *Figure 27* on page 10. Work the second section in same manner as the first except angle the strips in the *opposite direction*. If a paper base is used, remove the paper before sewing the long strips together to complete the project. When sewing sections together, alternate the slanted direction of the strips to make the *Chevron* design as shown in *Chevron Diagram 3.*

STRING DESIGNS ON A TRIANGLE BASE

String Pyramids

Shown in color on the back cover.
Block Size: Approximately 4¼″ high × 5″ wide at base.

String Pyramids is an old pattern, discovered in a collection of quilts from Utah which date back to the 1890's. This simple string triangle can utilize the smallest of your scraps and can be set in many different ways to form interesting allover patterns. Strips of string pyramids alternating with solid blocks can be set together in various ways; see the photograph and the Assembly Diagram for two examples. String pyramids can also be joined to form a hexagon as shown below.

Trace the pattern given on the next page and make a triangle template following the directions on page 4 — Template Supplies. Use the template to cut bases from paper or fabric. Cut strings from fabric from ½″−1″ width. When stitching strings to the base, start at one edge and work toward the other. Stitch the first string in place, right side up; stitch all other strings to preceding string and base with right sides facing, then turn and press to the right side before attaching new strings. When block is completely covered, turn to wrong side and trim away excess fabric; see *Figure 27* on page 10. Make several pyramids, then experiment with various settings before choosing the final assembly method.

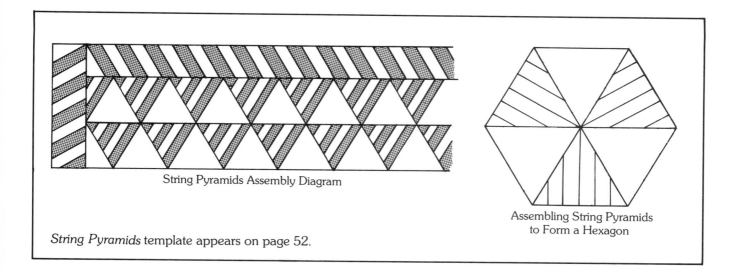

String Pyramids Assembly Diagram

Assembling String Pyramids
to Form a Hexagon

String Pyramids template appears on page 52.

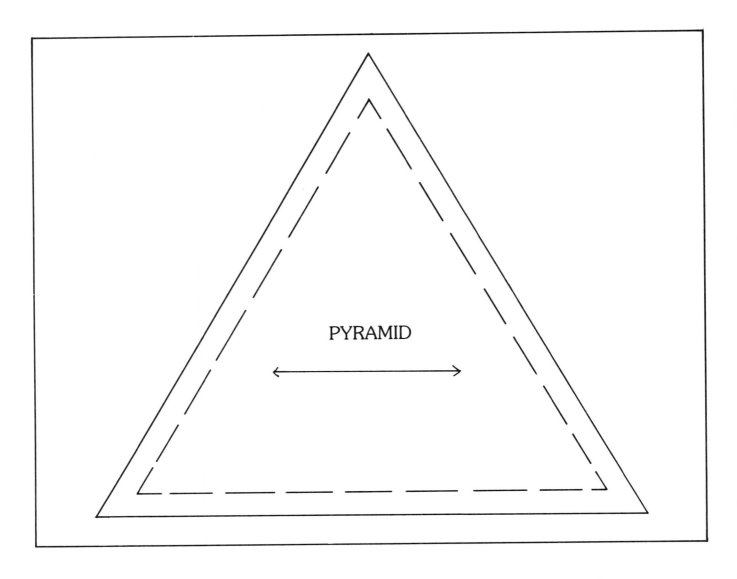

PYRAMID

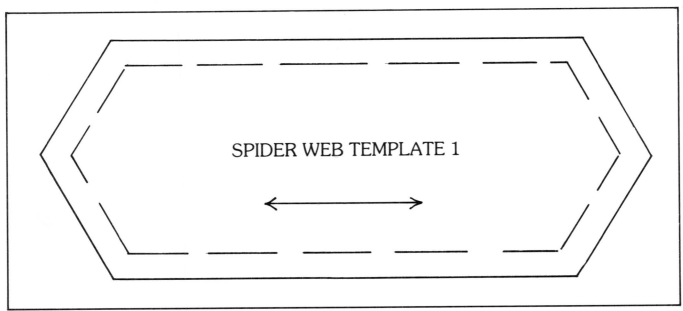

SPIDER WEB TEMPLATE 1

Spider Web

Block Size: Approximately 11½″ in diameter.

Spider Web is a striking design that can be made quite simply by one of the two methods given below. Four different but coordinating fabrics are needed to create each block; one of the fabrics should be a solid color for the center section (template 1—page 52).

Method 1: Following the directions on page 4—Template Supplies, make templates 1 and 2 using the patterns given on pages 52 and 54. Template 2 is a triangle; see note on the pattern. Mark and cut 2½″-wide strips from the solid fabric following *Figure 2* on page 6; mark and cut template 1 from the 2½″-wide strips as shown in *Spider Diagram 1*. Cut 1¼″-wide strips from the three other fabrics; cut out fabric strips in a proportion of 2:2:1 since two of the fabrics are used four times in the same section and one of the fabrics is used only twice. Following *Spider Diagram 2*, sew strips together; make all arrangements exactly alike. Using template 2 and following *Spider Diagram 3*, mark and cut triangles from the pieced strips. Sew one pieced triangle to each side of piece 1, forming a diamond shape.

Method 2: Following the directions on page 4—Template Supplies, make templates 1 and 3 using the patterns given on pages 52 and 54; template 3 is a diamond and will be used as the base. Mark and cut 2½″-wide strips from solid fabric following *Figure 2* on page 6; mark and cut template 1 from the 2½″-wide strips as shown in *Spider Diagram 1*. Use template 3 to cut bases from paper or fabric. Position piece 1 on base, right side up; stitch in place ⅛″ from edges. Using the sew-and-cut method of assembly (see page 13), stitch strips to each side of piece 1 in the order given, trimming, turning and pressing strips to right side after each addition; refer to *Spider Diagram 2* for the order in which the strips should be added to each side of piece 1. Turn base to wrong side and trim strips even with edge after diamond is completed; see *Figure 27* on page 10. If paper base was used, gently tear away paper at this time.

After diamonds have been made using one of the methods described above, sew diamonds together in groups of three forming a hexagon as shown in *Spider Diagram 4;* try to match like strips when sewing diamonds together. Sew hexagons together to form the *Spider Web* design as shown in the *Spider Web Assembly Diagram;* when many hexagons are joined, the solid template 1 pieces give the effect of borders on the edges of the webs.

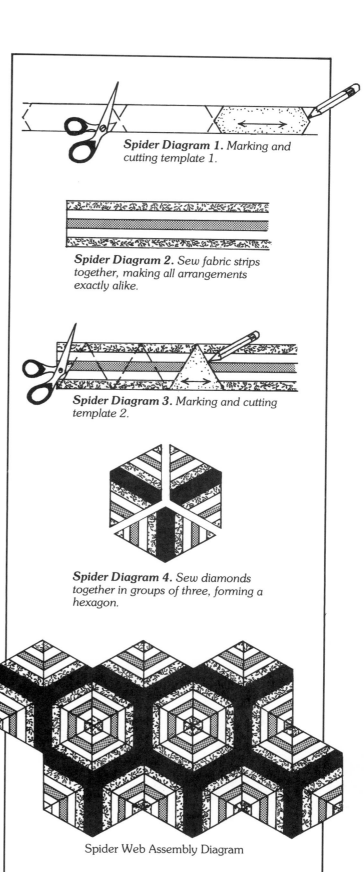

Spider Diagram 1. *Marking and cutting template 1.*

Spider Diagram 2. *Sew fabric strips together, making all arrangements exactly alike.*

Spider Diagram 3. *Marking and cutting template 2.*

Spider Diagram 4. *Sew diamonds together in groups of three, forming a hexagon.*

Spider Web Assembly Diagram

Spider Web templates appear on pages 52 and 54.

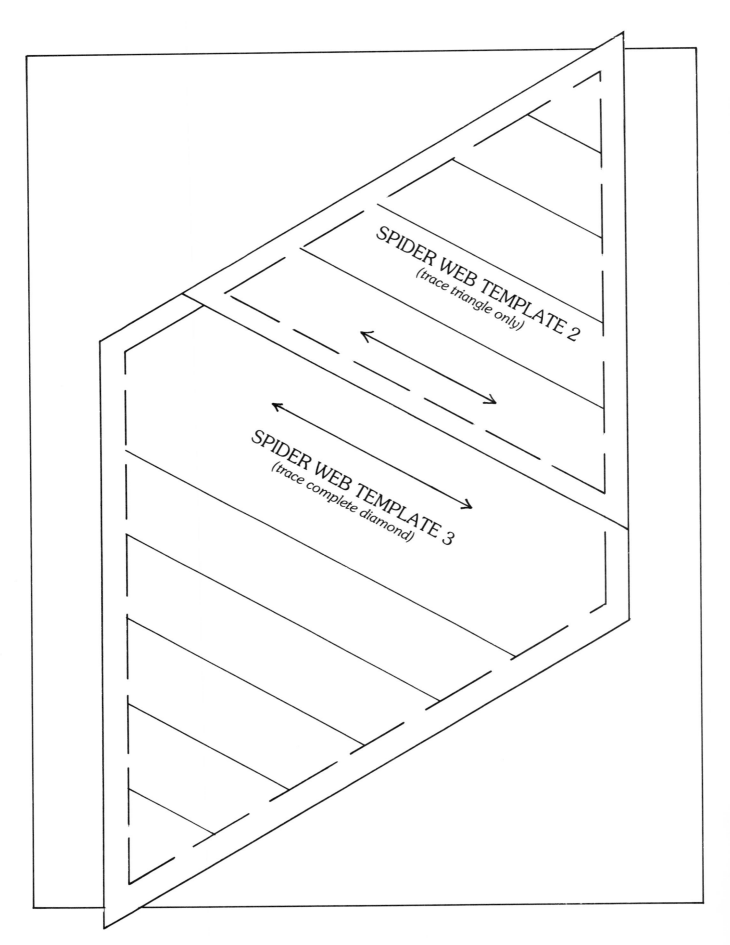

SPIDER WEB TEMPLATE 2
(trace triangle only)

SPIDER WEB TEMPLATE 3
(trace complete diamond)

Cobweb

Shown in color on the inside back cover.
Block Size: 17″ square.

This intricate-looking design can be made by sewing strips to a triangle base or by making string material (see pages 6–9) and using the triangle template to cut out eight sections. A template is given for the corners, which are added after the block is assembled to form a square.

Trace the patterns given on the next page and make two templates following the directions on page 4 —Template Supplies. Use one of the following methods to construct the eight sections of the *Cobweb:*

Method 1: Construct string material following the directions on pages 6–9; the material must be at least 6½″ high and 48″ wide to accommodate all eight sections. (The string material can be made in two 24″ sections, but make sure the strings are assembled in the same order to get the round *Cobweb* effect seen in the photograph.) Use template 1 to cut eight triangles from the string material. You will end up with two groups of eight triangles which are *exactly* opposite one another in strip arrangement; separate the groups and assemble only *like* triangles together to obtain the traditional *Cobweb* effect. For the corners, construct string material at least 3⅛″ high and 24″ wide. Use template 2 to cut four triangles from the string material; again, you will end up with two groups of opposite triangles. Divide the triangles into two groups; use one group for each block.

Method 2: Use template 1 to cut eight triangles from paper or fabric. Cut six different fabrics into strips 1½″ wide. Starting at the tip of the first triangle, stitch the first fabric strip—right side up and ⅛″ from the edges—to the base as shown in *Cobweb Diagram 1.* Following *Cobweb Diagram 2,* stitch the second strip in place with right sides facing; press to the right side after stitching. Continue in this manner until the entire base is covered. When base is completely covered with strips, turn to the wrong side and trim away excess fabric even with the base; see *Figure 27* on page 10. Repeat this procedure for the other seven triangles, stitching strips to each base in the same order as the first. Use template 2 to cut four corner triangles from paper or fabric. Stitch strings to each of the four corners in the same manner, again keeping the same order of application.

After making eight triangles and four corners by one of the methods described above, stitch one corner each to four triangle pieces with right sides facing and raw edges even, making ¼″ seams. Stitch the eight sections together, alternating plain sections and sections with corners to form a square.

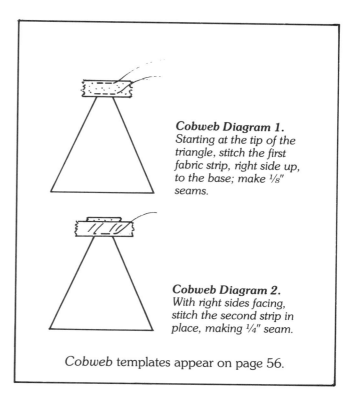

Cobweb Diagram 1.
Starting at the tip of the triangle, stitch the first fabric strip, right side up, to the base; make ⅛″ seams.

Cobweb Diagram 2.
With right sides facing, stitch the second strip in place, making ¼″ seam.

Cobweb templates appear on page 56.

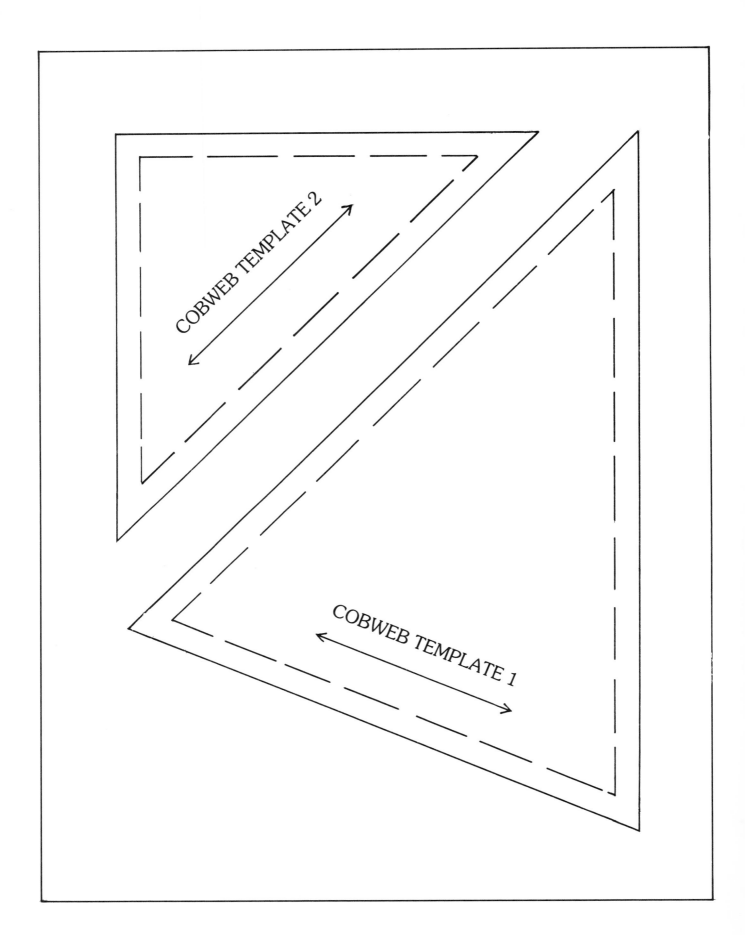

COBWEB TEMPLATE 2

COBWEB TEMPLATE 1

String Star

Shown in color on the inside front cover.
Block Size: Approximately 16⅝″ square.

The ever-popular star takes on new verve and energy when made of strings. To make up the star, eight diamonds are pieced with strings of various widths and colors—a great way to use up scraps. This is a good design for rotating your strips while sewing (see *Figure 15* on page 8) to create interesting angles as shown in the photograph. The diamonds are pieced together, then solid triangles and squares are added to create a complete block.

Select cottons in bright colors, prints and solids for the strips used on the diamonds. An interesting effect is obtained by beginning and ending the points of the diamonds with black. Use a solid color for the fill-in squares and triangles in a shade to match your decor. One beautiful version of this design had the eight diamonds constructed identically with the same widths of light and dark color bands; the fill-in squares and triangles were black, creating a dazzling spider web effect. Stripping can be used between the blocks, or blocks can be set side by side to form secondary designs.

Trace the patterns given on pages 58–59 and make one template for each following the directions on page 4 —Template Supplies. Use template 1 to cut eight diamonds from paper or fabric. Cut strips of various widths from bright solids and prints. Following *Figures 23–27*

on pages 9–10 for technique, stitch strips to each diamond, starting in center and working out toward each edge. Trim away excess fabric even with base as shown in *Figure 27*. If paper base was used, gently tear away paper at this time. Use template 2 to cut four triangles from solid background fabric. Use template 3 to cut four squares from background fabric.

Sewing eight sections together without puckering the fabric at the center can be tricky; follow these directions carefully to make the job easier: Mark seam lines and dots for beginning and end of seams on all pieces. Sewing is done from dot to dot, not from edge to edge of fabric. For the last half of each seam near the center, increase the seam width very slightly inside the marked seam line. Sew the sections together in four pairs, matching marked seam lines and dots, and beginning and ending stitching at dots. Sew pairs together to make two halves. Pin halves together, matching all seams at center and baste, then stitch. For the final joining, you may prefer to hand-sew for accuracy. Check to make sure a small hole is not left at center; if hand-sewing, a backstitch at center dot will help secure the edges. On wrong side, trim points ¼″ away from center joining. Fan out seams to reduce bulk, then press.

In same way, mark seams and dots of templates 2 and 3; fill in outside edges of star with those templates to form a square as shown in the photograph, again stitching from dot to dot rather than from edge to edge. Pin and stitch one edge of each template at a time to prevent puckering. Press carefully.

String Star templates appear on pages 58–59.

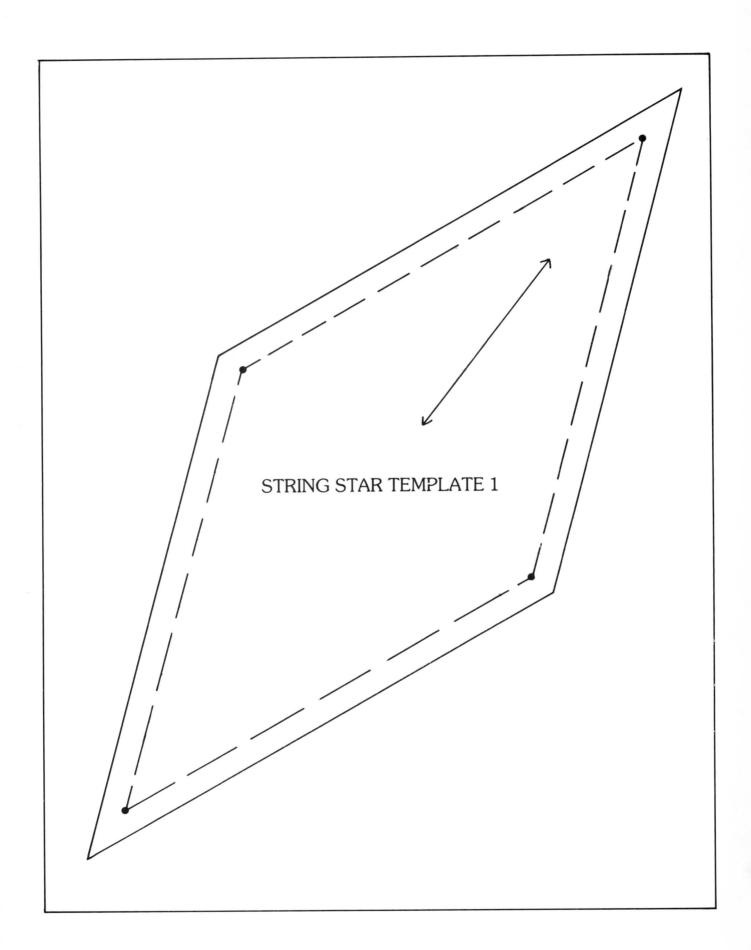

STRING STAR TEMPLATE 1

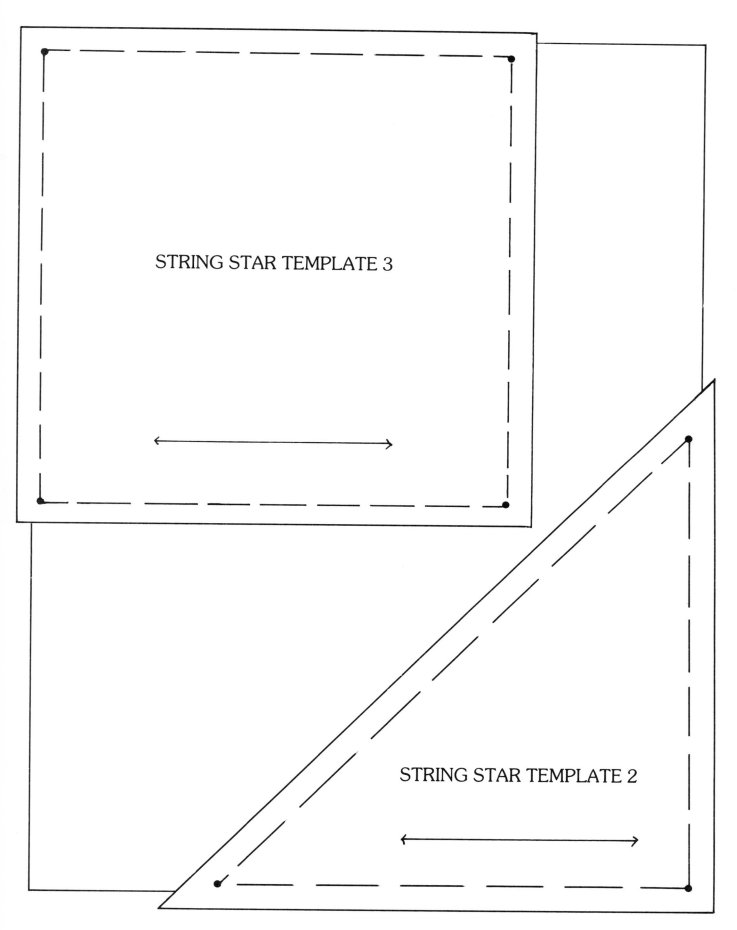

STRING STAR TEMPLATE 3

STRING STAR TEMPLATE 2

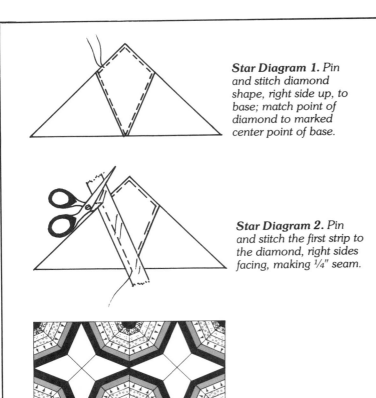

Star Diagram 1. *Pin and stitch diamond shape, right side up, to base; match point of diamond to marked center point of base.*

Star Diagram 2. *Pin and stitch the first strip to the diamond, right sides facing, making ¼″ seam.*

Stars and Spider Webs Assembly Diagram

Stars and Spider Webs

Shown in color on the inside front cover.
Block Size: 15″ square.

The beauty of this design becomes evident when four or more blocks are joined. Two separate shapes emerge: stars and spider webs.

For a startling yet lovely effect, make each block exactly the same using a solid bright color for the "stars" (diamond template) and coordinating fabrics for the strips. See the color photograph for a color suggestion. Choose one or two bold fabrics to use next to the diamond; these fabrics will "outline" each spider web. When purchasing fabrics for the strips, allow more fabric for the strips close to the diamond; the amount of fabric needed decreases for the strips at the outer edges.

Cut one 16″ × 16″-square base from paper or fabric. Fold in half twice on the diagonal and cut into four triangles; mark the center point of the longest edge of each triangle. Trace the diamond pattern given on the next page and make a template following the directions on page 4—Template Supplies. Use the template to cut four diamonds from the solid bright color you have selected. Cut all fabric strips 1¾″ wide and the width of the fabric.

Following *Star Diagram 1,* pin and stitch diamond shape, right side up, to base making ⅛″ seams; match point of diamond to center point of base as shown. With right sides facing, pin and stitch the first strip (the outer edge of the spider web) to the center diamond following *Star Diagram 2;* make ¼″ seam and trim away excess fabric. Turn and press to the right side, then add a second matching strip to the other side of the diamond in same manner; stitch in place. Continue adding strips alternately to each side of the diamond until the base is covered, turning and pressing after the addition of each strip. When base is completely covered, turn to wrong side and trim away excess fabric even with the base. Cover the other three triangle bases in same manner. Stitch the four triangles together as shown in the *Stars and Spider Webs Assembly Diagram,* making ¼″ seams and matching strips carefully.

For a 60″ × 75″ quilt, construct 20 blocks as described above; stitch together, matching strips, to form the *Stars and Spider Webs* design.

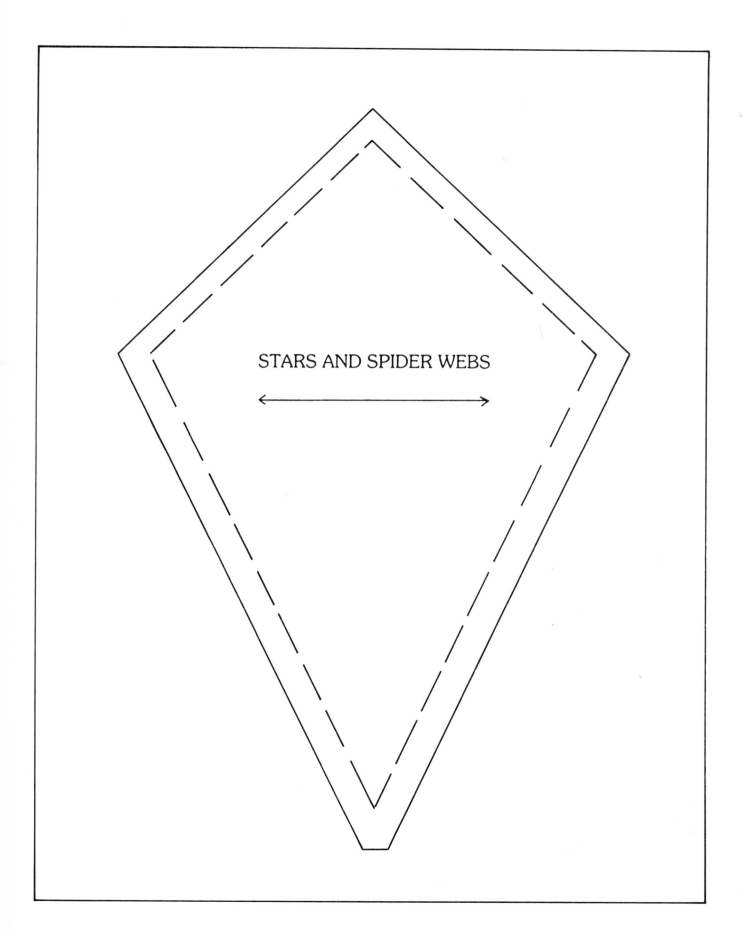

STARS AND SPIDER WEBS

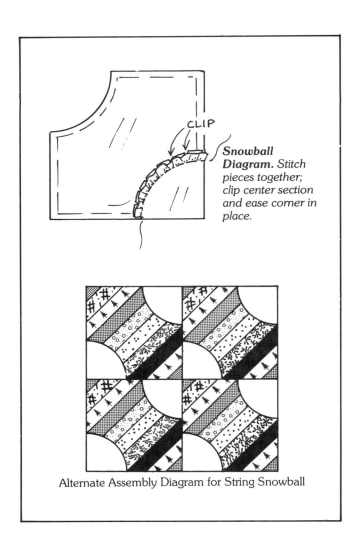

Snowball Diagram. *Stitch pieces together; clip center section and ease corner in place.*

Alternate Assembly Diagram for String Snowball

String Snowball

Shown in color on the inside front cover.
Block Size: 12″ square.

This old-fashioned design is also known as *Steeple Chase, Bows and Arrows* and *Boston Puzzle* when the center section is constructed from strings. I have used two colors for the corner sections to create an interesting effect when four 6″ units are joined; if one color is used for all corner sections, a perfect circle will be formed in between sections of strings.

Trace the patterns on the next page and make one template for each following the directions on page 4 — Template Supplies. Use template 1 to cut a base from paper or fabric. Cut strips of various widths from bright solids and prints. Following *Figures 23–27* on pages 9–10 for technique, stitch strips to the curved base, starting in center and working out toward each edge. Trim away excess fabric even with base as shown in *Figure 27.* If paper base was used, gently tear away paper at this time. Use template 2 to cut two corners from solid fabric; the same solid fabric is used for each corner in the same block. Clip the curved edges of center section. Carefully pin corner and center section together, easing corner into center section as shown in the *Snowball Diagram.* Stitch together making ¼″ seam. Press seam allowance toward corner. Repeat for opposite side of square. Press carefully. Make a second square as described above, then make two more squares using a different solid fabric for the corners; see color photograph. Join squares together to make one 12″ block following the photograph or the *Alternate Assembly Diagram for String Snowball.*

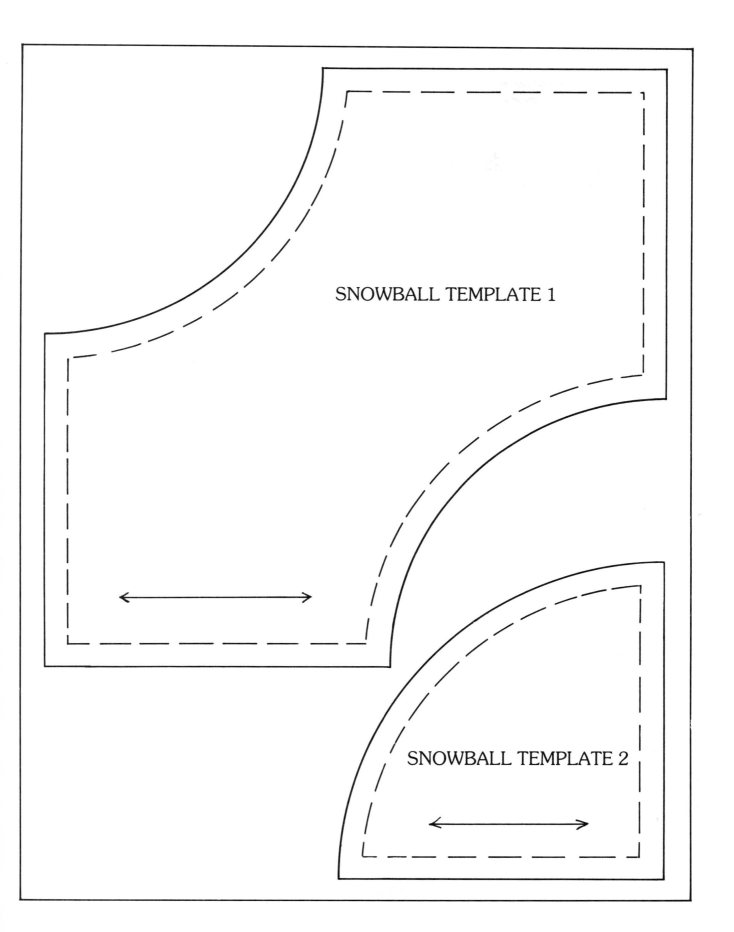

SNOWBALL TEMPLATE 1

SNOWBALL TEMPLATE 2

Metric Conversion Chart

CONVERTING INCHES TO CENTIMETERS AND YARDS TO METERS

mm — millimeters   cm — centimeters   m — meters

INCHES INTO MILLIMETERS AND CENTIMETERS
(Slightly rounded off for convenience)

inches	mm		cm	inches	cm	inches	cm	inches	cm
⅛	3mm			5	12.5	21	53.5	38	96.5
¼	6mm			5½	14	22	56	39	99
⅜	10mm	or	1cm	6	15	23	58.5	40	101.5
½	13mm	or	1.3cm	7	18	24	61	41	104
⅝	15mm	or	1.5cm	8	20.5	25	63.5	42	106.5
¾	20mm	or	2cm	9	23	26	66	43	109
⅞	22mm	or	2.2cm	10	25.5	27	68.5	44	112
1	25mm	or	2.5cm	11	28	28	71	45	114.5
1¼	32mm	or	3.2cm	12	30.5	29	73.5	46	117
1½	38mm	or	3.8cm	13	33	30	76	47	119.5
1¾	45mm	or	4.5cm	14	35.5	31	79	48	122
2	50mm	or	5cm	15	38	32	81.5	49	124.5
2½	65mm	or	6.5cm	16	40.5	33	84	50	127
3	75mm	or	7.5cm	17	43	34	86.5		
3½	90mm	or	9cm	18	46	35	89		
4	100mm	or	10cm	19	48.5	36	91.5		
4½	115mm	or	11.5cm	20	51	37	94		

YARDS TO METERS
(Slightly rounded off for convenience)

yards	meters	yards	meters	yards	meters	yards	meters	yards	meters
⅛	0.15	2⅛	1.95	4⅛	3.80	6⅛	5.60	8⅛	7.45
¼	0.25	2¼	2.10	4¼	3.90	6¼	5.75	8¼	7.55
⅜	0.35	2⅜	2.20	4⅜	4.00	6⅜	5.85	8⅜	7.70
½	0.50	2½	2.30	4½	4.15	6½	5.95	8½	7.80
⅝	0.60	2⅝	2.40	4⅝	4.25	6⅝	6.10	8⅝	7.90
¾	0.70	2¾	2.55	4¾	4.35	6¾	6.20	8¾	8.00
⅞	0.80	2⅞	2.65	4⅞	4.50	6⅞	6.30	8⅞	8.15
1	0.95	3	2.75	5	4.60	7	6.40	9	8.25
1⅛	1.05	3⅛	2.90	5⅛	4.70	7⅛	6.55	9⅛	8.35
1¼	1.15	3¼	3.00	5¼	4.80	7¼	6.65	9¼	8.50
1⅜	1.30	3⅜	3.10	5⅜	4.95	7⅜	6.75	9⅜	8.60
1½	1.40	3½	3.20	5½	5.05	7½	6.90	9½	8.70
1⅝	1.50	3⅝	3.35	5⅝	5.15	7⅝	7.00	9⅝	8.80
1¾	1.60	3¾	3.45	5¾	5.30	7¾	7.10	9¾	8.95
1⅞	1.75	3⅞	3.55	5⅞	5.40	7⅞	7.20	9⅞	9.05
2	1.85	4	3.70	6	5.50	8	7.35	10	9.15

AVAILABLE FABRIC WIDTHS

25"	65cm	50"	127cm
27"	70cm	54"/56"	140cm
35"/36"	90cm	58"/60"	150cm
39"	100cm	68"/70"	175cm
44"/45"	115cm	72"	180cm
48"	122cm		

AVAILABLE ZIPPER LENGTHS

4"	10cm	10"	25cm	22"	55cm
5"	12cm	12"	30cm	24"	60cm
6"	15cm	14"	35cm	26"	65cm
7"	18cm	16"	40cm	28"	70cm
8"	20cm	18"	45cm	30"	75cm
9"	22cm	20"	50cm		